I love cookbooks, I've got loads of them at home, but this is one of
the best ones I've ever seen!

Ian Dempsey, *Today FM*

At last, a book for people who are scared of cookery books. Simple,
easy recipes that are healthy and interesting. Donal Skehan's book
reclaims good food from the convenience of supermarket shelves
and puts it back where it belongs – in the domestic kitchen.

Paolo Tullio, *Irish Independent* and *The Restaurant*

Donal is one of a breed of wonderful new chefs whose love affair
with home cooking has burst from the kitchen counter ... onto the
bookshelf.

The Irish Examiner

Spreads the gospel of healthy home-cooked food.

The Irish Tatler

MERCIER PRESS

Cork

www.mercierpress.ie

Trade enquiries to CMD BookSource, 55a Spruce Avenue, Stillorgan Industrial Park, Blackrock, County Dublin

© Donal Skehan, 2009

ISBN: 978 1 85635 629 9

10 9 8 7 6 5 4 3 2

A CIP record for this title is available from the British Library

Photos: Donal Skehan, Jocasta Clarke (pp. 4, 42, 44, 62, 66, 72, 74, 90, 110, 126, 136, 140, 148, 156, 162, 164, 174, 178, 200, 234, 244, 246, 248, 252), Aoife Nathan (pp. 6, 14, 18, 30, 31, 32, 34, 36, 40, 70, 144, 196, 204, 208, 240)

Food Styling: Erica Ryan and Donal Skehan

Printed and bound in the EU.

GOOD MOOD FOOD

Simple Healthy Homecooking

DONAL SKEHAN

MERCIER PRESS
IRISH PUBLISHER – IRISH STORY

Contents

Calming and Nutritious Dinners 145

Introduction

About Good Mood Food

My lifelong dream was to have my own kitchen, and when I moved into my first flat, I couldn't keep myself out of it. It was the process of having to cook dinner for myself every day which made me realise how much I loved the actual process of cooking and everything that came with it. I couldn't wait to get home from work to create my next dish, try a new ingredient, add a new spice – the kitchen became my playground and my guests, my guinea pigs! Not that they were complaining.

I started 'the Good Mood Food blog' in 2007 and it came about as the result of one simple thing – I have a terrible habit of cooking a really tasty dish, but forgetting to write down ingredients. With so many recipes being cooked, I started 'the Good Mood Food blog' as a means of recording what I was cooking. But I never imagined the worldwide community I would be joining in doing so. All of a sudden people were commenting on my recipes, telling me what they liked and disliked, and what they would add and remove. In turn I would visit their blogs, which were packed full of unknown culinary delights and inspiration from across the globe.

In January 2008 I received an email from Mercier Press discussing the possibility of developing a cookbook based on the blog. Within a few months we were putting ideas together for a book! The recipes are based around the way I cook and hopefully will provide you some really easy meals which are full of flavour and bursting at the seams with nutritional value. I hope you enjoy making the recipes from *Good Mood Food* as much as I have writing the book and if nothing else, I hope it leaves you full!

About Me

Throughout my life, I have always been surrounded by homemade fresh food, so when it came time to move out on my own for the first time, I couldn't imagine living life without it.

I grew up in Howth, a fishing village just outside Dublin, and as a kid one of my favourite things to do was to bake. I got such enjoyment out of producing something from a combination of ingredients which looked so completely different from their original state. My best friend and I used to hawk our creations to our poor neighbours who must have been driven mad with us knocking on their doors to sell them our produce for far more than it was worth!

The transition to cooking real meals came after I spent a summer in France with an old family friend. My mom had prepped me with five fool-proof recipes which I had been practising and, on pain of death, I was to cook for the family! I was sent off with a hug, a kiss and a side of smoked salmon from the west pier in Howth, which was my mom's standard gift for foreign friends. However, after a long flight and a hot and sticky drive through the south of France, I ended up with a whole suitcase of clothing smelling of smoked salmon that lingered for the rest of the summer!

As a willing guest, I sampled everything that was put in front of me, from classic French home-cooked dishes like Beef Bourguignonne and effortless yet elegant fresh green salads lightly dressed, to the simplicity of wafer-thin smoked ham and melon slices, a concept completely foreign to me as an Irish twelve-year-old. I was hooked!

Another turning point in my experiences with food came during my teens, when I was introduced to the Asian market in South Great Georges Street, Dublin. I discovered an array of incredible and fascinating foreign ingredients, with which completely unfamiliar dishes could be created. A pocket-sized Asian recipe book from my granny allowed me to work my way through recipes, from simple stir fries to Nasi Goreng, even making my own fortune cookies.

Nothing made me happier than watching other people eating the food I had created and more importantly enjoying it.

One of my first cheffing experiences was with the well-established Reveljen restaurant in Gothenberg, Sweden. They ran a unique and traditional Christmas Smorgasbord on Elfsbog Fastning, the island which sits just at the entrance of Gothenburg Harbour. My task was to churn out traditional Swedish Christmas dishes by the truckload – the island catered for staff Christmas parties and saw guests being ferried across from the mainland. During their journey over, they were numbed to the rough seas by the popular Christmas drink, Glogg. As you can imagine they were ready to eat by the time they arrived! The owners ran the whole event like a military operation, and even though I may not have been cooking *haute cuisine*, the kitchen skills and discipline that were drilled into us was absolutely invaluable.

Healthy Eating
Survival Guide

Good Mood Food
Healthy Eating
Survival Guide

Eating healthily for me is not just about following the latest diet fad, or becoming a health extremist, it's about choosing good quality, fresh ingredients, preparation, and most of all enjoyment!

As simple as it may sound, a good breakfast, lunch or dinner has the potential to turn your day around, affecting energy levels and mood.

For me, the basics of any good diet and balanced lifestyle come down to four simple guidelines:

- Eat fresh foods: Eating foods which are as close to their natural state as possible, has to be the number one way of providing the body with a wide array of vitamins and minerals.

- Eat a variety of foods: Keeping your system active is essential. By choosing from a range of food groups, you stimulate a more healthy digestion and continuously challenge your body.

- Eat by colours: One of the simplest ways of knowing you're choosing the right foods is to eat by colours. Most fruit and vegetables are bursting with colour and are packed with antioxidants. Not only will they be appealing to your stomach, the bright colours will also stimulate your appetite!

- Keep hydrated: making sure to drink an adequate amount of water should be a big priority, but is also something that many people forget (8 glasses of water a day is generally recommended).

Following these few steps will have you prepared for a lifetime of healthy eating. I think preparation is the key to successful healthy eating. Going to the supermarket or shops without a clear idea of what you need or want can be one of the biggest mistakes made. Unnecessary items will always find their way into your basket.

Leave the house with meal ideas in your head, a good solid list of what you need and stick to it! Doing this will not only allow you to save money, it also means less waste, and you won't be tempted to buy items not on the list. Forget the biscuits two-for-the-price-of-one, get in, get the stuff and get out!

Of course, you don't have to go to extremes and write a menu plan for the week, but having some key ingredients in your kitchen helps to prevent any unhealthy food choices. It also means that even when you're not at your most motivated you can still rustle up something quick, satisfying and healthy.

I have listed a lot of the ingredients used in this cookbook and ones which I buy regularly for my kitchen. If you have a well-stocked kitchen, you should be able to throw together a quick pasta dish, a tasty meat marinade, or even a quick salad without batting an eyelid!

My Store Cupboard Essentials

Oils: Extra Virgin Olive Oil, Olive Oil, Sunflower Oil, Sesame Oil.

Vinegars: Balsamic, Red Wine, White Wine, Rice Wine.
(These all help to make fantastic dressings, or marinades for meat.)

Mustards: Dijon, Wholegrain, English Mustard Powder.
(Each of these mustards can really enhance the recipe they are added to.)

Sea Salt Flakes.
(These are a must; aside from the crunch factor they give a much better flavour than the finer table salt.)

Flour: Plain White, Self-Raising, Wholemeal, Oat.
(Oat flour is a great addition to your store cupboard; it can easily be made by whizzing up rolled oats in a food processor.)

Pasta: Spaghetti, Penne, Tagliatelle, Rigatoni and Couscous.
(Try to choose wholewheat where possible. Wholewheat pasta provides a much more substantial carbohydrate than its refined version, and will keep you going that extra bit longer!)

Honey.
(I use honey whenever I can. It works great in marinades, baking and in teas.)

Peanut Butter.
(Apart from lashing it on some toast, peanut butter can add a great nutty taste to noodle sauces, cookies and even in smoothies.)

Tahini Paste.
(This is a smoky paste made from sesame seeds; there are two types, light and dark, I generally go for the lighter version.)

Noodles: Buckwheat Soba Noodles, Rice Vermicelli, Egg Noodles.
(Head out to an Asian market and pick up a wide selection of different noodles, there is a huge variety so try them all.)

Tinned Goods: Whole Plum Tomatoes, Chopped Tomatoes, Chickpeas, Butter Beans, Kidney Beans, Black-Eyed Peas, Sweetcorn.

(I can't sleep at night without knowing I have a tin of chopped tomatoes in my cupboard! Tinned goods can be transformed into simple dishes so easily: a tasty tomato sauce, fresh houmous, homemade beans-on-toast, a hearty soup – there are so many options!)

Dried Goods: Vegetable Bouillon Powder, Good Quality Beef Stock Cubes, Bulgar Wheat.

(Marigold is an excellent brand of Vegetable Bouillon Powder.)

Rice: Wholegrain Basmati, Japanese Sushi Rice.

(There are many different rices to choose from, but for normal rice dishes I tend to use wholegrain basmati. It has a different, more earthy flavour than the white version. It can take a bit of getting used to, but it is a lot healthier for you in the long run.)

Soy Sauce, Thai Fish Sauce (Nam Pla), Oyster Sauce.

(These are my Asian cupboard staples, you can use them in so many dishes. I would be lost without them!)

Rolled Oats.

(If there is one ingredient you have to add to your diet it is rolled oats. They are a super, super, superfood! Packed with nutrients and health benefits, they are a slow releasing carbohydrate full of fibre.)

A wide selection of nuts and seeds: Sesame, Pumpkin, Sunflower, Walnuts, Pine, Brazil, Almonds, Hazelnuts.

(Picking up a good selection of nuts and seeds has become so easy these days, with most supermarkets producing their own little packets. Nuts and seeds are one of the best plant sources of protein.)

Raisins.

(Great to use in homemade mueslis and desserts, and baked in muffins.)

Tabasco Sauce.

(Just a drop of this stuff can really add a nice kick of heat to tomato sauces.)

Also a quick note on the recipes in this book: I use goat's milk quite a bit, but feel free to substitute regular milk if you so wish.

My Freezer Essentials

Even at your most organised there will always be days where the couch looks a hell of a lot more tempting than heading into the kitchen to create a culinary masterpiece.

Using your freezer successfully can be a fine art! Filling it with the right stuff can make sure you are never more than just a few steps away from a tasty tomato sauce, a delicious soup, or even a fruit smoothie. Here is my list of essential freezer stand-bys/staples:

- **Red Wine**
I always fill ice cube trays with the remains of wine bottles. You can add them straight to sauces to give them a rich deep flavour.

- **Garden Peas**
Of all the frozen vegetables, peas are one of the big success stories. Frozen peas are great to use in soups, rice dishes, and even as an extra vegetable portion.

- **Chicken Stock**
Homemade chicken stock is a freezer must-have. I make a huge pot of this after a roast chicken and divide the stock into freezer bags, perfect for adding to soups.

- **Mixed Berries**
I use frozen berries quite a lot. They come in packs which are easy to pick up and stick straight in the freezer for smoothies or even a tasty dessert.

- **Poultry and Meat portions**
Frozen poultry and meat portions can make life a lot easier. Simply take out the portions the morning you want to use them, stick them in the fridge and by the time you come home for dinner they are ready to use.

- **Basic Tomato Sauce**
I love knowing I have a few portions of tomato sauce in the freezer. It means that you will always be one step away from a simple bolognaise, an easy pasta dish, or even a homemade pizza.

Basic Tomato Sauce

Making a great tomato sauce can take around 30 minutes and it can be the base of so many dishes. Even if I'm making it to use straightaway, I always make more than I need so I can freeze the extra portion.

Serves 4–5 as a pasta sauce

2 x 400g tins chopped tomatoes
75ml/3fl oz red wine
1 large onion, finely chopped
2 garlic cloves, finely chopped
1 tablespoon of olive oil
1 teaspoon of dried oregano
A generous pinch of sea salt and ground black pepper

- In a large frying pan, heat the olive oil and fry the garlic and onion until soft.
- Add the oregano, salt and pepper and stir through. Add the chopped tomatoes and red wine to the rest of the ingredients. If you don't have wine to hand, you can substitute it with the same amount of water. This will work just as well, but the red wine gives a richer flavour to the sauce as it reduces.
- Bring the sauce to the boil, then reduce the heat and simmer for about 20 minutes or until the sauce has thickened.
- Make sure to stir the sauce every few minutes while it's cooking.
- Use straightaway, or allow to cool, divide into resealable freezer bags and pop in the freezer.

Basic Chicken Stock

The beauty of a good hearty chicken stock is that not only is it packed with health benefits, but it can be the base for hundreds of different, quick and simple recipes.

Makes approximately 12 pints

Leftover bones and carcass of chicken
6 litres/12 pints water
350ml/12fl oz white wine
1 white onion, chopped
1 large carrot, sliced
1 large leek, sliced
1 stick of celery, chopped
3 stalks of parsley
8 black peppercorns

- Place the chicken bones, carcass and the rest of the ingredients in a large pot with the water and bring slowly to a steady boil.
- Allow to simmer for 3 hours or until the flavour is right for you.
- Make sure to check on the pot every now and then, to skim any fat and scum that rises to the surface – this will ensure you have a nice clear stock.
- Strain the stock and allow to cool.
- The stock can be kept in the fridge for a few days or frozen in handy bags in the freezer.
- You can also store some of the liquid in ice cube trays, which comes in handy to add an extra bit of flavour to sauces and gravy.

Grow your own herb garden

Grow your own herb garden

Growing herbs is so simple. Even with limited space it's possible to produce a variety of stunning herbs which will add an extra depth and freshness to any recipe. Pick up a few pots and plants at your local garden centre to start your very own herb garden. Here is a list of the basic herbs you can easily grow at home:

- **Basil**

This can be grown quite easily at home: stick the plant on a sunny windowsill with lots of light and make sure to snip off the top leaves every now and then, and water regularly.

- **Mint**

Mint is a tough plant which will take over your garden if you plant it alongside other herbs. I grow my mint in its own little pot and it thrives the whole year round.

- **Thyme**

Thyme is really easy to grow and adds amazing flavour to certain dishes.

- **Rosemary**

Rosemary is a super herb, which goes great with roast meat and vegetables. The plant itself is quite hardy and should last the whole year round. To harvest, snip off at the woody stems.

- **Oregano**

Oregano is a more gentle herb, which tends to die off in the winter but magically appears again in the late spring/early summer. It has a really aromatic flavour to it, and goes great in tomato sauces and Italian dishes.

- **Sage**

My sage plant at home has taken off and produces really big leaves perfect for harvesting. Sage is wonderful with meat and pasta or used sparingly in stocks and soups.

- **Parsley**

Parsley is an old favourite and can be used in so many dishes. It's an extremely

easy herb to grow and it grows quite rapidly. Both the stalks and the leaves can be eaten. I find curly leaf parsley easier to grow than flat leaf as it is a lot hardier.

Unused or leftover herbs can be stored as herb butters – just mix chopped herbs with butter, roll and wrap in cling film and store in the fridge or freezer.

Drying herbs is another method which can really bring out some intense flavours from the plants and they can often be even tastier than their fresh counterparts. They are a fantastic addition to recipes and I love using them to intensify the flavours of soups, stews and sauces. Hardy herbs like thyme, rosemary, oregano, bay and sage are perfect for drying and in most cases the natural oils are not depleted during the process.

Try to harvest the herbs on a dry day, mid morning just after the dew has dried. This will ensure the herbs are at their freshest when you pick them.

Here are my tips for harvesting and drying herbs:

- Snip the herbs at the stem.
- Choose nice long branches and pick off any dead leaves.
- Give the stems a gentle shake to remove any insects or dirt. (You can choose to give the herbs a quick wash, but make sure to dry on kitchen paper, as moisture can cause rot.)
- Bundle a good handful of the stems together and tie at the bottom with twine tightly. As the herbs dry, you may need to tighten the knot.
- Hang the herbs in a warm dry place. I hang mine in a small room just over the water heater, so they're kept nice and warm.
- The time it takes to dry the herbs will depend on their moisture content, but in most cases when the stems crack and no longer bend, they are ready to be stored.
- Store the dried herbs in an airtight container and leave the leaves uncrushed until you're ready to use them.

Enjoy the herbs right through the winter and give your dishes some extra flavour!

Wash your own salad leaves!

The convenience of picking up a pre-washed bag of designer salad leaves has quickly become commonplace in our modern lives. However, the gases and chemicals sometimes used in the production of these bags, can leave a residue of unnecessary toxins which our bodies can seriously do without. A normal salad leaf will last about 3–4 days in the fridge whereas some of these cut salad leaves can continue looking fresh in the bag for a whopping 10 days. That just can't be right!

There is nothing more satisfying than preparing your own salad leaves; it's a much greener kitchen practice and it tastes so much better.

There are so many exciting salad leaves you can choose from, all at really reasonable prices. My standard mix is a combination of frisee and oakleaf. But there are so many more, such as Lolla Rossa, Baby Gem, Curly Endive, or Cos, so be adventurous – it'll make the difference when it comes to dishing up. Here are my quick and simple steps to preparing salad:

- Fill your sink with cold water.
- Remove any packaging and cut out the core or separate the leaves from the stem.
- Submerge the leaves in the water and give them a good swill, allow to sit for about 10 minutes. (This will allow dirt to settle to the bottom, and the cold water will bring wilted leaves back to life.)
- Take a handful of leaves out of the water at a time and spin in a salad spinner until they are completely dry. (Moisture is not your friend here as it will shorten the life of the stored leaves, so make sure they're dry.)
- Store the leaves loosely in a dry tea towel, or in an airtight zipper bag in the bottom crisper drawer of your fridge. The leaves should last between 3–4 days depending on the leaf.

And that's it, a few simple steps for healthy salads all week long. It's so worth it, and once you start, you will never go back to soggy bags of gas flushed leaves again!

Cleansing Food

Cleansing Food

Let's face it, we all go through patches of unhealthy eating and times when we may overindulge.

The good news is that nature provides us with the best antioxidants, vitamins and minerals on the planet. These can be found in fruit, vegetables and many common herbs. By including just a few simple cleansing ingredients bursting with the good stuff, you will not only give your system a mini spring clean, but you will feel better for it.

Eating meals which are full of cleansing fruit and vegetables can really put you right back on track. Sometimes it can be as easy as including a couple of standard ingredients in your meals.

Juicing has to be the ultimate way of giving your body a great spring clean and a nutritious kick. Choose a good brand of juicer, and one that is easy to clean: you should be able to stick most of the parts into the dishwasher and give the rest a rinse under a tap.

Although it's a little bit of hassle, juicing does have its benefits and the endless choice of healthy drinks it produces is well worth it. With so many tasty combinations you can have lots of fun experimenting. I normally use a mixture of carrots and apples as a base to experiment with. This sweet combination almost always makes adding a vegetable like broccoli a lot more manageable.

I have included a few different combinations here, but do try juicing different vegetables with the carrot and apple mix, until you get a little bit braver!

Apple, Carrot and Ginger Juice

One of my favourite juices has to be this one and the addition of ginger gives it a real zing!

Makes 2 glasses

3 apples, cored
2 carrots, topped and tailed
1 thumb-sized piece of ginger, peeled

- Depending on your juicer you may have to chop your ingredients and remove the apple cores. I like to leave the skin on and just give them a good rinse under the tap. Prepare the ingredients and blitz them in the juicer. You should end up with a lovely frothy juice. Serve with a few ice cubes.

Celery, Carrot and Apple Juice

Celery can be a fairly demanding in juice and can be a little bitter, which is why I like to include it with this apple and carrot mix.

Makes 2 glasses

2 stalks of celery
2 carrots, topped and tailed
3 apples, cored

- Drop all the ingredients into the juicer and serve the tasty frothy juice with a few ice cubes. Drink straightaway.

Apple, Pear, Ginger and Cinnamon Juice

This juice always reminds me of Christmas and cold winter mornings, I guess it's the dash of cinnamon.

Makes 2 glasses

2 apples, cored

1 pear, cored

1 thumb-sized piece of ginger, peeled

½ teaspoon of ground cinnamon

- Prepare all the fresh ingredients and pass them through the juicer. Pour the juice into a small jug and sprinkle with the cinnamon powder. Using a spoon, stir in the cinnamon powder. Pour the juice into two large glasses and serve immediately.

Mango, Banana and Blueberry Smoothie

I love smoothies any time of the day and this mix is particularly tasty.

Makes 2 glasses

1 mango

2 bananas

100g/3½oz blueberries

Orange juice

A handful of ice cubes

- Slice the mango in three, avoiding the large flat stone in the centre; score the flesh on the two sides in a criss-cross pattern, and push the skin inside out. You should now be able to cut the pre-sliced chunks straight off. Add the chunks to a blender with the ice cubes, bananas and blueberries. Pour in enough orange juice to cover the fruit and ice. Blitz in the blender until smooth and serve straightaway.

Super Green Broccoli and Spinach Soup

This is my super green soup. It's packed with great ingredients, and best of all it's 100% healthy! If you don't have fresh spinach, frozen spinach will work just as well.

Serves 4

1 medium head of broccoli, stalk removed
3 large handfuls of fresh spinach
2 leeks, finely chopped
2 stalks of celery, finely chopped
1 litre/2 pints vegetable stock
1 tablespoon of olive oil
A generous pinch of ground black pepper
Sea salt to season

- In a large pot heat the olive oil and fry the leeks with the black pepper for 2 minutes, or until they soften.
- Add the celery, broccoli, and spinach and cook for a further 3 minutes. Don't be put off by the amount of spinach, once the heat gets at the leaves, they will quickly wilt.
- Add the vegetable stock and salt and bring to the boil, reduce the heat and cook at a steady simmer for 20–25 minutes, or until the broccoli is soft when pierced with a fork.
- Remove from the heat and blitz with a hand blender until the soup is smooth.
- Add further seasoning if required and serve straightaway.
- Alternatively you can allow the soup to cool and divide into individual resealable plastic bags for the freezer.

Boot Camp Soup

This a surprisingly tasty soup, which is wonderfully cleansing. Used originally as part of a weight-loss diet, I make it regularly as a really substantial lunch. This recipe makes a generous amount — I freeze half the soup and keep the rest in the fridge.

Serves 8

3 onions, chopped into chunks
2 green peppers, chopped into chunks
1 bunch of celery, chopped into chunks
1 iceberg lettuce, chopped into chunks
2 x 400g tins chopped tomatoes
800ml/1½ pints vegetable stock
300g/10½oz lentils or soup mix
Sea salt and freshly ground pepper

- Add all the ingredients to a large pot and bring to the boil. Reduce the heat and simmer for 20–30 minutes until the lentils are soft.
- Blend the soup to a smooth consistency with a hand blender; you may need to add a little extra stock if the soup is too thick. Season with salt and pepper, and serve.

Ginger, Lemon and Honey Tea

If you change one thing in your life, change how you drink tea. There are so many options out there nowadays it's a crime to just stick to the usual milk and two sugars. Teas are a great way to get the system going in the morning. Even hot water with lemon juice can be a great kick start to clear out your gut! This ginger, lemon and honey tea is my get-well-soon remedy which I always drink at the first sign of the sniffles.

1 thumb-sized piece of ginger
Juice of ½ lemon

1 teaspoon of honey
Boiling water

- Peel the ginger and slice into thin oval discs. Place in a big cup and drizzle over the honey and lemon juice. Fill the cup with boiling water and allow to steep for 3 minutes before drinking.

Orange, Mint and Lemon Balm

There is another great dose of vitamin C in this tea. I grow my own lemon balm, quite successfully, in a little flowerpot on my windowsill. You can easily pick up one of these amazingly fragrant plants at any good garden centre. It's a hardy little herb which is said to have many stress-reducing and calming properties.

Juice of 1 orange
6 mint leaves

6 lemon balm leaves
Boiling water

- Use the end of a wooden spoon to crush the mint and lemon balm leaves in the bottom of a large cup. Or you can give them a bash in a pestle and mortar to release their natural oils.
- Add the orange juice and fill the cup with boiling water. Allow to steep for 3 minutes.

Breakfast

Breakfast

So many people forget about breakfast, but when your mother told you to eat it, she was right! I will admit that I am one of those annoying morning people, so for me breakfast has to be one of the best meals of the day, providing an opportunity to start the day correctly. You know when you get it right, because you feel like you can conquer anything! Time is always one of the key factors when it comes to eating in the morning and breakfast can quite easily become one of the most commonly skipped meals.

However, breakfast does have the potential to be one of the most exciting meals of the day, and with a little preparation it truly can be. Make the time in the morning to sit down and eat, and your body will thank you for it.

Included here are some of my favourite breakfast recipes, which are so tasty that you won't have a hard time making a habit of eating every morning. Porridge is one of my favourite breakfast foods when I have time, and I have included my favourite apple and cinnamon porridge recipe here, but you can do so many things with this dish – try adding fresh fruit, a quick drizzle of honey, or even a fresh smoothie stirred through. Be adventurous and experiment!

Of course there will always be mornings when you just don't have the time to sit down, so for those of you who need something to grab and run I have included some handy breakfast snacks to eat on the go. Healthy muffins and breakfast bars are always a great solution, and try sticking a smoothie in one of those fancy thermos coffee mugs for a super tasty breakfast.

Blueberry and Banana Muffins

Muffins are perfect for eating on the go. These blueberry and banana muffins are packed with healthy ingredients, which will keep you going for any busy morning.

Makes 12 muffins

125g/4½oz blueberries
2 bananas, mashed
125g/4½oz plain flour
75g/3oz wholemeal flour
200g/7oz rolled oats
75g/3oz brown sugar
250ml/8½fl oz milk
2 large eggs, separated
3 tablespoons of sunflower oil
3 teaspoons of baking powder
1 teaspoon of cinnamon
1 teaspoon of salt

- In a large mixing bowl, combine the flour, rolled oats, baking powder, cinnamon, salt and sugar.
- Create a well in the dry ingredients and add the banana, egg yolks, milk and oil. Mix everything gently until a wet batter forms.
- In a separate bowl, whisk the egg whites until they form soft peaks. Fold the egg whites and blueberries into the muffin batter until everything is mixed evenly.
- Divide the muffin mix into individual paper cases and place in an oven for 25 minutes at 200°C/400°F/Gas Mark 6.
- The muffins should be fine to eat for 4–5 days and can easily be frozen in zip lock bags.

Apple and Oatmeal Muffins

These muffins are great for breakfast, packed with fibre and are simple to make – they're even easier if made the night before.

Makes 8–10 muffins

2 eating apples, grated
100g/3½oz raisins
90g/3½oz rolled oats
150g/5oz wholemeal flour
90g/3½oz brown sugar
200ml/7fl oz goat's milk
1 egg
2½ teaspoons of baking powder
¼ teaspoon of salt
¼ teaspoon of cinnamon

- Preheat the oven to 200°C/400°F/Gas Mark 6.
- In a large mixing bowl mix the flour, oats, sugar, baking powder, salt and cinnamon.
- With a wooden spoon, make a well in the centre of the dry mix and add the egg and milk. Gradually incorporate the dry ingredients to form a thick, wet mixture.
- Fold in the grated apple and raisins.
- Using a dessertspoon, spoon even amounts of the mixture into baking cases in a muffin baking tray.
- Sprinkle with a little extra rolled oats and place in the oven for 25–30 minutes.
- These are great to stick in the freezer in resealable bags. Perfect to take out the night before you want to use them.

Apple and Cinnamon Porridge

The rolled oats used in porridge have recently been recognised as one of the easiest and most accessible superfoods. I'm sure that every house has their own way of cooking porridge and mine seems to change depending on my mood. A rushed morning can see it cooked in the microwave with a little bit of honey and water but, on the days I do have time, this how I do it:

Makes 2 portions

250g/9oz rolled oats
480ml/16fl oz goat's milk or water
1 large apple, grated
A good dusting of cinnamon powder
A drizzle of honey to taste

- The best thing about this little mix is the texture of the cold sweet tangy apple against the creamy porridge. Perfect for slurping down on a cold morning. Make sure to grate the apple just before you serve, otherwise it will start to brown.
- In a small pot, combine the milk and the oats and place over a medium heat, stirring continuously. It usually takes about 10 minutes to get the right consistency.
- To the pot add the grated apple and stir through. Sprinkle with cinnamon, drizzle with honey and serve straightaway.
- A great start for breakfast, now you can go and enjoy the day.

Mixed Berry and Banana Smoothie

Berries are another widely celebrated health food, providing a good source of antioxidants which help the body fight disease. Unless you have the ingredients in the kitchen, smoothies are very hard to conjure up on their own. Frozen berries actually produce a perfectly chilled drink without the addition of ice and a smooth texture.

Makes 1 glass

100g/3½oz mixed frozen berries
1 banana
Orange or apple juice (not from concentrate)

- Allow the berries to thaw slightly before putting them into a food processor. Add the banana and fill the container up as far as the berries with orange or apple juice.
- Then blend and serve, it's really quick and really easy.

Big Kid Peanut Butter and Banana Smoothie

This is my big kid treat when it comes to smoothies and it generally raises a few eyebrows. It tastes a whole lot better than it sounds, just make sure you use smooth peanut butter and not chunky, that's not a mistake I ever want to repeat!

Makes 2 glasses

2 tablespoons of smooth peanut butter
1 tablespoon of organic yoghurt
2 bananas

A handful of ice cubes
Orange juice

- Throw the bananas in a blender; add the peanut butter, organic yoghurt, ice cubes, and enough orange juice to cover the mix. Whizz up until smooth and serve straightaway.

Oat Pancakes

This is really tasty alternative to regular American-style pancakes, and includes one of my biggest health food discoveries: oat flour! It is so simple to make. Pile a portion of rolled oats into a food processor and whizz it until it becomes fine. The flour gives a mellow sweet taste to the food it is used in and is a great way to add extra fibre to recipes. This mix also works great for use on waffle irons.

Makes approximately 8–10 pancakes

100ml/4fl oz goat's milk
120g/4oz oat flour
2 large eggs, separated
1 teaspoon of baking powder
¼ teaspoon of salt
½ teaspoon of cinnamon

- Add all the dry ingredients to a large mixing bowl.
- Measure the milk in a jug and add the egg yolks. Whisk lightly to combine.
- Add to the dry ingredients and mix until blended.
- In a clean bowl whisk the egg whites until they hold firm peaks.
- Fold gently into the batter until combined.
- To cook simply add a heaped dessertspoonful of the mixture to a warm pan with a little butter; it takes approximately a minute each side or until golden brown.
- Serve with maple syrup, fresh fruit or whatever takes your fancy!

Homemade Nutty Breakfast Bars

This is a perfect solution for 'breakfast on the go'. I generally make these the night before to have alongside a smoothie in a thermos. The combination of nuts, oats and bran flakes makes this a perfect little snack not just for breakfast, but at any time during the day.

Makes 24 bars

75g/3oz almonds
75g/3oz hazelnuts
75g/3oz pumpkin seeds
125g/4½oz rolled oats
125g/4½oz bran flakes
200ml golden syrup
75ml maple syrup
2 tablespoons of honey
1 teaspoon of vanilla extract

- Whizz the almonds, hazelnuts and pumpkin seeds in a food processor for about 30 seconds. Toast them on a large roasting tray in an oven for 6–8 minutes at 200°C/400°F/Gas Mark 6, or until they turn nice and golden. Keep a keen eye on them! Take them out and set aside to cool on a plate.
- In a large mixing bowl, combine the rolled oats, bran flakes and toasted mixed nuts and seeds.
- In a small saucepan, bring the golden syrup, maple syrup, honey and vanilla extract to the boil and simmer for 3 minutes, or until it starts to thicken. Pour the mixture over the dry ingredients in the bowl and mix until everything is coated in the thick syrup.
- Press the mixture into a small 9-inch square baking tin with greaseproof paper, and pack tightly. Cover and place in the fridge until firm.
- Cut into breakfast bar pieces, wrap these up in greaseproof paper to go.

Baked Breakfast Eggs

This is well worth the effort for breakfast, the combination of flavours is great.

Makes 4 portions

4 free range eggs
100g/3½oz goat's cheese
2 large handfuls of fresh spinach
4 slices of cooked ham, diced
2 garlic cloves, finely chopped
1 tablespoon of olive oil
Pinch of sea salt and freshly ground pepper

- In a hot frying pan sauté the garlic for about 30 seconds in the olive oil.
- Add the spinach and keep moving around the pan until it has wilted and become soft.
- Remove from the heat and separate into four medium-sized ramekins.
- Top with a sprinkling of diced ham and a slice of good quality goat's cheese.
- Break an egg into each ramekin and season with sprinkle of salt and pepper.
- Bake in the oven at 200°C/400°F/Gas Mark 6 for 10–12 minutes or until the white of the egg is no longer transparent.
- Serve with some crisp bread to dip in the rich, runny yolk.

Easy Homemade Muesli

Forget all your designer mueslis offering low salt or low sugar. If you look further down the very same aisle in the supermarket you will find all the ingredients you need for your very own customised super-duper homemade muesli. This is my recipe, but there are so many other ingredients you can add, just let your mind run wild!

Makes approximately 8 servings

50g/2oz wheatgerm
50g/2oz bran flakes
250g/9oz rolled oats
50g/2oz sunflower seeds
100g/3½oz brazil nuts, roughly chopped
125g/4½oz raisins
50g/2oz ground flaxseeds

- Combine the ingredients and store in an airtight container.

Scrambled Eggs and Asparagus

When you do find time to have a cooked breakfast, this is a really tasty one. Versatile as eggs are, nothing seems to beat a good scramble. For me there is a certain sense of satisfaction when you place sophisticated asparagus spears on the plate for breakfast and a particular delight in slopping a good dollop of scrambled eggs on top. Regardless of how you feel eating it, it's easy and quick to make, and thanks to the asparagus, it's highly nutritious and bursting with Vitamin K, which is crucial for healthy bones.

Makes 2 portions

4 large organic free range eggs
About 12 asparagus spears
2 tablespoons of goat's milk
A good pinch of salt and pepper

- Break the eggs into a bowl and whisk together with the milk and set aside.
- Hold the asparagus with both your hands and bend it slightly, you should feel a natural breaking point (it should be about an inch from the bottom). At this point snap the woody ends off the asparagus. You can steam the asparagus spears or submerge in a pot of boiling, salted water and simmer for about 2 minutes or until tender.
- As the asparagus is cooking, scramble the eggs over a low heat, stirring continuously to make sure they do not stick.
- Working quickly, drain the asparagus and place onto a plate, and top with the scrambled eggs.
- Top with a sprinkle of salt and pepper and dig in!

Zingy Fruit Salad

Fruit salads are so simple to make, and with this ginger and lime juice dressing it's a real eye-opener for early mornings!

Makes 2 portions

1 red apple, chopped in chunks
A handful of fresh pineapple chunks
A handful of blueberries
A handful of fresh melon chunks
4 tablespoons of apple juice (not from concentrate)
½ thumb-sized piece of ginger, grated finely
Juice of 1 lime

- Add all the fruit to a large serving bowl.
- Add the apple juice, ginger and lime juice, and toss so that everything gets a nice gingery lime coating.
- Serve straightaway, or add a little homemade granola for an extra crunch.

Soft-Boiled Egg with Home Fries

These home fries are a delicious accompaniment to a perfectly soft-boiled egg. I first tried home fries in Florida where it came as part of the standard American breakfast, and although they were a little heavy to be eating so early in the day, they were delicious. Home fries can easily be adapted with whatever you may have in your fridge: add some bacon pieces, some finely chopped red pepper, or even some mushrooms. I generally boil the potatoes the night before, as the whole process can seem a little more work for a breakfast meal when it is done all at once.

Serves 2

3 large potatoes
1 tablespoon of sunflower oil
1 onion, finely chopped
2 eggs

- Chop the potatoes in half and place in a large pot with a lid. Cover the potatoes in water and bring to the boil over a high heat.
- When the potatoes come to the boil lower the heat so the water comes to a steady simmer and cook for 10–15 minutes or until the potato is tender when pierced with a fork. Drain the potatoes, allow to cool and carefully chop into bite-sized chunks.
- Chop the onion and gently fry in a large frying pan with a tablespoon of oil over a medium heat for about 2 minutes or until the onion softens and begins to take colour.
- Add the potato pieces and fry on all sides for about 6–8 minutes or until the pieces are all nicely browned.
- Place the two eggs into a small pot and cover with water and bring to the boil. When the water begins to boil, set a timer for 3 minutes.
- After 3 minutes drain the eggs under cold water and serve alongside a generous portion of home fries.

Cinnamon and Raisin Breakfast Bagels

I first tried these bagels in America and have been hooked ever since. The flavours are perfect for a cosy late morning breakfast. Bagels are really easy to make and if you can master bread making you can definitely give them a go.

Makes 12 Bagels

125g/4½oz raisins
500g/1lbs strong white flour
350ml/12fl oz lukewarm water
1 x 7g sachet dried yeast
3 tablespoons of sugar
1 tablespoon of cinnamon
2 teaspoons of salt
1 egg, beaten

- Soak the raisins in a bowl of boiling water for 30 minutes. Place the flour in a large bowl and make a well in the centre with the back of a spoon.
- Pour the water, yeast and sugar into the well and allow to sit for 6–8 minutes or until it becomes thick and frothy.
- Add the cinnamon and salt, and using a spoon slowly incorporate the flour into the yeast and water mix until you form a dough.
- Turn the dough out onto a floured surface and knead in the raisins.
- Continue kneading for 4–5 minutes until the dough becomes smooth and elastic.
- Grease the mixing bowl, place the dough in it and cover with a damp cloth.
- Leave in a warm place to rise for 30 minutes or until the dough has doubled in size.
- Punch the dough down and turn out onto a floured surface.
- With your hands shape the dough into a long sausage shape and cut into 12 pieces.

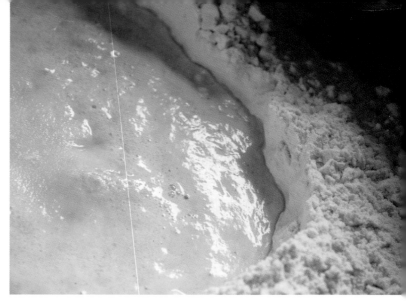
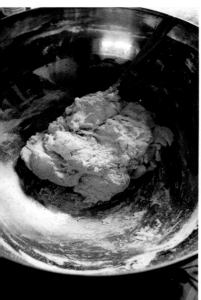

- Poke your finger through the middle and with your fingers form the bagel shape.
- Place on greaseproof paper and set aside for 5 minutes.
- Preheat the oven to 190°C/375°F/Gas Mark 5.
- Bring a large pot of water to the boil, lower the heat to simmer and put 4 bagels in at a time.
- Cook the bagels for approximately 1 minute either side, turning with a slotted spoon.
- Drain the bagels and place on a floured baking sheet. Brush with a little beaten egg and place in the oven for 20–25 minutes until they are golden.
- Enjoy toasted with a little butter.

Homemade Crunchy Granola

One of my worst habits when it comes to eating is getting comfortable with one recipe and repeating it again and again. This granola mix is a prime example, and I can go for weeks eating it religiously every day for breakfast and then not touch the stuff for months. But I always come back to it because it is such a great kick start to the day, with lots of healthy, nutritious ingredients. This mix in particular gives a lovely smoky taste to the oats and gets an extra little zing from the cinnamon powder. I have made this recipe to my taste, but you can add some extra nuts, seeds or dried fruits if you like. Keep an eye on the nuts and fruit in the oven, as they tend to cook that little bit quicker than everything else. Make yourself a big batch and keep it in an airtight container for a tasty breakfast.

Makes enough for 6-8 servings

250g/9oz jumbo oats
50g/2oz sesame seeds
50g/2oz sunflower seeds
125g/4½oz raisins
50g/2oz ground flaxseed and goji berry mix
1 tablespoon of honey
1 teaspoon of cinnamon powder
¼ teaspoon of salt

- Combine all the dry ingredients in a large mixing bowl, drizzle over the honey and mix through. Empty the contents onto a large baking tray and spread out evenly.
- Toast in the oven for approximately 20 minutes at 180°C/350°F/Gas Mark 4, but keep an eye on it as ovens vary – you are looking for the oats to just turn a light golden brown. Allow to cool before you transfer to an airtight container. The granola should last up to two weeks, if you don't eat it all before then!
- Serve with fresh goat's milk or some organic yoghurt and mixed berries.

Brunch, Lunch
and Munch

Brunch, Lunch and Munch

Eating the standard three meals a day is fine, but I always find my stomach rumbling after breakfast. Studies suggest that eating more regularly can improve our metabolism and it makes sense. Eating smaller and more regular meals throughout the day can prevent us experiencing the sluggish feelings after eating large meals, and the loss of energy experienced when we go without! With this in mind, I have put together some really tasty nutritional lunches and snacks which can be eaten throughout the day.

One of the main reasons I started eating five meals a day, apart from a rumbling stomach, was because, unless I had something prepared, I found myself skipping lunch. This is probably one of the worst things you can do, almost as bad as skipping breakfast! If you miss lunch, your body is forced to survive the day on what it has had for breakfast, assuming you ate breakfast.

The key when it comes to eating healthily throughout the day is preparation. If you know what you are having for lunch and plan for it, you will instantly avoid the classic mistake of trying to choose what to eat when you are hungry. The mind will always scream for the easy option, so take control.

It might take a little more time preparation in the evening, but don't leave home without a plan. It can be as easy as making a little extra portion when you're making dinner. Not only will you know what you're eating, but you will save a serious amount of cash too!

Get yourself excited about lunch again. Remember as a kid how exciting it was to show off a shiny new lunch box on your first day of school? Well channel that and go out and buy a fancy new lunch box or even a thermos flask. You might get funny looks from friends and co-workers, but hey you know deep down they're dead jealous!

My Top 5 Lunch Box fillers:

- Nuts and Seeds: There is a recipe for a **Nut Snack Mix** on page 135, but simply mix your favourite nuts and seeds together for the perfect little hit of nutrition. Throw in some raisins too.

- Soups: There are so many options for healthy soups, which is why they give you the perfect excuse to go out and buy a swanky new thermos flask!

- Chunky salads: Nice chunky cut salads, made from raw veggies like celery, broccoli, cabbage, and cucumber will hold really well tossed in a dressing until lunch time.

- Grains and roast vegetables: Stick on a big tray of roast veggies, drizzle with some olive oil and balsamic vinegar, boil up some rice, quinoa or lentils and mix the two together A match made in heaven!

- Wholewheat wraps: There are so many options when it comes to fillings for wraps. Fill the wraps with thinly sliced vegetables tossed in a tasty Asian dressing or use them to make tasty grilled vegetable quesadillas.

Irish Brown Yeast Bread

This has to be one of the easiest bread recipes in the world; with no kneading it's a no brainer. The loaf can be frozen and defrosted when needed and is the perfect accompaniment to a hearty soup or made into a chunky sandwich. For anyone hooked on white bread this is a much healthier alternative and you can also add rolled oats sprinkled on top for an extra crunch.

Makes 1 loaf

450g/1lb wholemeal flour
450ml/15fl oz warm water
1 x 7g sachet dried yeast
1 teaspoon of treacle
1 teaspoon of salt
A small handful of mixed seeds

- Mix the flour, salt and yeast in a large bowl. Dissolve the treacle in the warm water and add to the dry mix.
- With a large spoon combine the ingredients until they form a wet mixture.
- Turn the mixture into an oiled and floured 2lb-loaf tin (21cm x 11cm x 6cm), sprinkle with seeds and cover with cling film or a damp tea towel.
- Place in a warm spot to allow the yeast to do its work for approximately 20 minutes.
- Bake for about 45–50 minutes at 220°C/425°F/Gas Mark 7. You will know when the loaf is done when you insert a skewer and it comes out clean, or when it begins to shrink away from the edge of the tin.
- This bread is very moist and will last for up to a week. You can store it in an airtight container. It also freezes brilliantly for up to a month, so you could also make a few extra to save for later.

Bacon, Avocado and Sundried Tomato Sandwich

There are quite a lot of things that get me excited about food, but when it comes to sandwich ingredients, the combination of bacon and avocado always has me drooling! When I have time to eat at home for lunch this is one of my favourite sandwiches to make. Try and choose some tasty bacon from your butchers, it will make all the difference.

Makes 4 tasty sandwiches

4 slices of brown bread
1 nice ripe avocado
4 rashers of good quality bacon
75g/3oz sundried or sunblushed tomatoes roughly chopped
A pinch of sea salt and ground black pepper
A little butter to spread

- Place 4 rashers under a hot grill and cook on both sides till crispy.
- Toast 4 slices of brown bread.
- Slice the avocado in half, remove the stone and carefully scoop out the flesh.
- Slice the avocado into half moon pieces.
- Butter the slices of toast and place a rasher of bacon on each slice.
- Top the bacon with pieces of avocado and tomatoes.
- Sprinkle with a little sea salt and ground black pepper.
- Serve straightaway.

Simple Tuna Niçoise

Before a visit to the south of France, I had never tried a Niçoise salad, but now I'm a total convert. Try to use the eggs a few days after you buy them, they will be easier to peel.

Makes 4 portions

2 large tuna steaks

4 eggs

Approximately 16 baby potatoes

500g/1lb green beans, topped and
  tailed

1 small punnet of cherry tomatoes

4 baby gem lettuces

1 small red onion thinly sliced

A pinch of black pepper and sea salt

For the vinaigrette:

1 clove garlic crushed

3 tablespoons of extra virgin olive oil

1 teaspoon of dijon mustard

1 tablespoon of red wine vinegar or the
  juice of ½ lemon

- Place the potatoes in a pot and cover with boiling water, bring back to the boil and simmer for 10–12 minutes or until tender. Rinse under cold water and cut each potato in half. Set aside.
- Place the green beans in a pot of salted boiling water and cook for 2 minutes. Drain in a colander and rinse with cold water. Set aside.
- Season the tuna steaks with black pepper and cook on a hot pan for 2 minutes each side. Remove from the heat and slice into thin strips.
- Place the eggs in a small saucepan and cover with water. Bring to the boil and simmer for 4–5 minutes. This will produce soft-boiled eggs, if you want hard-boiled, simply double the time. Remove and place eggs in cold water, to prevent them cooking further. When cooled, roll on a flat surface applying slight pressure so the shell cracks, and peel. Set aside.
- While the eggs are cooking, add the ingredients for the vinaigrette to the bottom of a large salad bowl and give a quick whisk. Slice the cherry tomatoes in half and tumble into the bowl. Separate the leaves of the baby gem lettuces and roughly tear into the salad bowl. Slice the red onion and add to the bowl with the green beans and potatoes. Toss all the ingredients in the vinaigrette, making sure everything is nicely coated.
- Divide the salad onto serving plates. Halve the eggs and place on top of the salad with the tuna steak strips and a sprinkle of sea salt.

Mediterranean Roast Vegetables with Bulgar Wheat

Roast vegetables are delicious enough to be eaten on their own with just a little sea salt, but pair them up with some bulgar wheat and you have the makings of a really delicious meal. You can use any roast vegetables here, carrots, beetroot or asparagus all work, but I really love the combination of aubergine, courgette, red onion and red pepper.

Makes 4–5 generous portions

1 aubergine
2 courgettes
2 red onions
1 red pepper
200g/7oz bulgar wheat
Enough boiling water to cover the
  bulgar wheat

1 teaspoon of vegetable bouillon
  powder
2 tablespoons of olive oil
A good pinch of sea salt and ground
  black pepper

- Place the bulgar wheat in a large bowl and cover with boiling water.
- Stir through the vegetable bouillon powder, cover with a cloth or cling film and allow to sit for about 30 minutes or until all the water is soaked up.
- Preheat the oven to 200°C/400°F/Gas Mark 6.
- Chop all the vegetables into bite-sized chunks. Add to a large bowl and toss with the oil, sea salt and black pepper.
- Arrange the vegetables on a large shallow non-stick roasting tray, making sure not to overcrowd it, as this will make the vegetable pieces become soft.
- Place the roasting tray in the oven for approximately 30–40 minutes or until the vegetables become slightly charred on the edges.
- Remove the tray from the oven and allow to cool.
- Add the roast vegetable pieces to the bulgar wheat and stir gently to combine.
- You may want to season with a little extra sea salt and black pepper at this point.
- Serve the bulgar wheat as a tasty side dish or use as a super lunch box filler.

Tzatziki Lamb Koftas

You can't go wrong with this little dish, I first tasted the wonderful combination of minced lamb with dried oregano on holidays in Turkey as a kid. Restaurants there cook the little lamb patties on long skewers and serve them with tasty fresh salads. This recipe doubles up as a great lunch box filler — for easy transportation, mix the lamb and tzatziki together and roll up in some soft wholemeal tortilla wraps.

Serves 4

500g/1lb lamb mince
1 onion, finely diced
2 tablespoons of fresh parsley
Ground black pepper and sea salt
½ head red cabbage, shredded thinly
2 teaspoons of Worcestershire sauce
2 teaspoons of dried oregano
4 wholemeal pitta breads

For the Tzatziki:
1 cucumber
200g/7fl oz Greek yoghurt
2 tablespoons of extra virgin olive oil
Juice of ½ lemon
10 mint leaves, finely chopped
2 garlic cloves, finely chopped
Ground black pepper and sea salt
Pinch of paprika

- In a bowl, combine the lamb mince with the Worcestershire sauce, dried oregano, onion, parsley, salt and pepper. Get your hands in there and give the mixture a good squeeze. Form palm-sized patties of the mince and place on a plate, cover with cling film and pop in the fridge while you get on with the tzatziki.
- Slice the cucumber in half and with a small spoon scoop out the seeds and discard. Chop the cucumber into nice thick half moon slices, and place in a bowl. Spoon the Greek yoghurt on top of the cucumber and dress with olive oil, lemon juice, mint, garlic, salt, black pepper and a pinch of paprika. Combine all the ingredients so the cucumber is nicely coated. Cover the bowl and stick in the fridge.
- Place the lamb koftas under a hot grill and cook for 3–4 minutes on both sides.
- Serve the koftas in wholemeal pitta pockets with a generous serving of tzatziki and shredded red cabbage.

Easy Antipasto Salad

This little antipasto salad is my simple solution to any pre-dinner nibbles. Three tasty ingredients combine to make a delicious starter which can be thrown together in no time at all. This is a great base for any salad, so feel free to throw in some lovely extras if you wish. Things like toasted pine nuts, garlic croutons and sundried tomatoes would all work great in this. If you buy olives unpitted, simply crush them with the back of a knife and remove the stone with your fingers.

Serves 4

3 large handfuls of rocket leaves
50g/2oz green olives (pitted)
1 packet Parma ham slices
A large handful of wafer-thin parmesan cheese slices
3 tablespoons of extra virgin olive oil
1 tablespoon of balsamic vinegar
A small pinch of ground black pepper

- The method for this one is so easy – simply mix together the olive oil, balsamic vinegar and black pepper in a large mixing bowl.
- Arrange the remaining ingredients on a serving plate.
- Drizzle over the dressing and serve. Make sure to provide lots of crusty bread to eat alongside and enjoy!
- To be honest, this is more of a sit down affair, but if you did want to transform this dish into proper finger food, simply toast some small slices of bread, spread with a little pesto, wrap a few rocket leaves, wafers of parmesan cheese and crushed olives in some Parma ham slices, place on the pesto toast and hold together with a cocktail stick.

Spicy Gazpacho Salad

When it comes to salads, this little number beats them all hands down! Combining all the tastes and flavours of Gazpacho soup, it is packed with nutrition and full of crunch. I sometimes make this as a party snack too. Get your hands on a packet of little baby gem lettuce heads, break off the leaves and fill with tablespoons of the salad and top with the dressing. Perfect healthy finger food!

Serves 4

6 large tomatoes, chopped coarsely
1 cucumber, roughly chopped
1 large red onion, roughly chopped
4 celery stalks, roughly chopped
2 red peppers, roughly chopped
1 head cos romaine lettuce, roughly torn
3 tablespoons of extra virgin olive oil
Juice of ½ lime
1 teaspoon of Tabasco sauce
A large handful of freshly chopped parsley
1 tablespoon of red wine vinegar
2 wholegrain crisp breads, crumbled

- Add the olive oil, lime juice, Tabasco sauce and red wine vinegar to a large mixing bowl and whisk to combine.
- Add all the vegetables and parsley to the bowl.
- Season with ground black pepper and coarse sea salt, and toss the salad until everything is coated.
- Serve on a bed of roughly torn cos romaine lettuce and top with crumbled crisp breads.

Sesame Chicken Satay Skewers

These chicken skewers are perfect for party snacking, but also go really well with a nice leafy green salad for a tasty lunch.

Serves 4

4 free range chicken breasts
200ml/7fl oz of coconut milk
1 garlic clove, finely chopped
½ red chilli finely chopped
1 thumb-sized piece of ginger, finely grated
1 tablespoon of sunflower oil
3 tablespoons of soy sauce
2 tablespoons of tahini paste
Juice of 1 lime
A handful of toasted sesame seeds

- Cut the chicken breasts into long strips lengthways and thread onto skewers. Cover and set aside in the fridge.
- In a small saucepan, fry the garlic, chilli and ginger in the sunflower oil for 30–40 seconds.
- Add soy sauce, tahini paste, coconut milk and lime juice and bring to the boil.
- Reduce the heat and allow to simmer, stirring until the sauce thickens. Remove from the heat and set aside.
- Heat a griddle pan, brush the chicken skewers with oil and then fry them for 2–3 minutes each side.
- Remove from the heat and place on plates. Drizzle over the satay sauce and top with a sprinkling of toasted sesame seeds.

My Favourite Couscous

If you have never made couscous before, this is the perfect recipe to try. It has to be one of the simplest ingredients to cook and can be transformed in so many ways. This is the recipe I always use for couscous, but stick in any other fresh vegetables you like and feel free to experiment.

Serves 4

225g/8oz couscous
100g/4oz feta cheese, crumbled
425ml/¾ pint vegetable stock
1 red onion, finely chopped
½ cucumber, chopped into rough chunks
A large handful of flat-leaf parsley, roughly chopped
A handful of basil leaves, roughly chopped
A good handful of mixed seeds, toasted
Juice of 1 lemon
3 tablespoons of extra virgin olive oil
Sea salt and black pepper

- Prepare the couscous according to the instructions on the packet. As a general rule, soak it in twice its volume of stock for ten minutes and then simply fluff up with a fork once it has absorbed the water.
- Prepare the rest of the ingredients and mix together in a large bowl. Add the couscous and combine all the ingredients.
- Serve straightaway, or cover and keep in the fridge as a tasty little meal to snack on.

Spicy Chicken and Cucumber Salad

This is a really fresh and spicy-tasting salad which will definitely clear those sinuses! You can easily prepare this recipe ahead of time: cook the chicken, prepare the salad and dressing, and when it comes time to serve simply combine all three. If you don't have all the ingredients to hand for the dressing it's not the end of the world. Even a dash of sesame oil and lime juice can really bring the flavours to life.

Serves 2

2 chicken breasts, finely sliced
2 tablespoons of oat flour to coat the
   chicken slices (or wholemeal flour
   will work just as well)
½ cucumber, finely sliced lengthways
6 radishes, finely sliced
1 red onion, finely sliced
2 red peppers, finely sliced
A good pinch of salt and pepper
A little sunflower oil for frying

For the dressing:

2 tablespoons of sunflower oil
Juice of 1 lime
1 tablespoon of rice wine vinegar
1 tablespoon of fish sauce
1 teaspoon of sesame oil
½ red chilli, very finely chopped
2 garlic cloves, very finely chopped
1 thumb-sized piece of ginger, peeled
   and very finely chopped

- Mix the flour with a little salt and pepper and coat the thinly sliced chicken.
- Heat some oil and fry the chicken in a hot pan with until nice and brown, then set aside.
- For dressing, in a large bowl, combine the oil, lime juice, rice wine vinegar, Thai fish sauce (Nam Pla), sesame oil, garlic, chilli and ginger. This should be to your taste so add something, subtract something – be my guest!
- Add the cucumber, radish, red onion and red pepper to the bowl. Mix all the ingredients together in the spicy dressing.
- Serve the spicy cucumber salad with the chicken strips on top and enjoy.

Spinach and Potato Frittata

This was my mom's quick answer to a meal when she had nothing ready for dinner and we knew it! Not that we complained though, this all-in-one pan dish is really filling and the combination of eggs, spinach and garlic is always a winner. This recipe works best using a 24cm frying pan, this produces the right thickness. Using a bigger pan means the frittata will be spread too thinly. For an extra hit of saltiness, crumble some feta cheese over the frittata just before it goes under the grill.

Serves 2

3 medium potatoes
4 eggs, lightly beaten
1 teaspoon of butter
1 garlic clove, finely chopped
1 onion, finely sliced
A large handful of spinach, washed and dried
A good pinch of sea salt and black pepper
A pinch of paprika

- Boil the potatoes until tender, rinse under cold water and, when they are cool, slice thinly (about a ½cm) and set aside.
- Melt the butter in a hot pan and add the garlic and onion and cook for 2–3 minutes or until they become golden and tender. Add the spinach, cook until wilted and spread evenly across the bottom of the pan.
- Arrange the slices of potato on top of the spinach. Season beaten eggs with a pinch of black pepper and paprika.
- Pour the eggs evenly over the potatoes, onions, garlic and spinach. Give the pan a gentle shake to allow the eggs to surround the ingredients. Cook over a gentle heat until the mixture has set around the edges, but is still a little soft in the centre. Season with salt and pepper.
- Pop the whole pan (be careful of plastic handles!) under a hot grill to finish cooking for about 2 minutes or until nicely browned.
- Slice into chunky wedges and serve with a side salad. Any leftovers make a tasty little breakfast the next morning, hot or cold.

Asian Shitake Noodles

I love these noodles so much! I will happily admit that I wasn't always a fan of shitake mushrooms, knowing them only in their dried form. However, I recently picked up a little punnet of these Asian mushrooms, used them in a stir fry and I was converted. Shitake mushrooms have been used in Chinese medicine for over 6,000 years because of their many health-promoting properties. Research has linked them with immune-boosting benefits and the ability to help fight viruses. I suggest buckwheat soba noodles here, but you can easily use egg noodles or whatever you have available. If you visit an Asian food store you should find a wide array of different and interesting noodles to choose from. Go wild!

Serves 2 generous portions

250g/9oz buckwheat soba noodles
1 garlic clove, finely chopped
1 red chilli, deseeded and finely chopped
2 shallots, finely sliced
2 small carrots, finely sliced
1 tablespoon of sunflower oil

A large handful of shitake mushrooms, sliced thinly
3 tablespoons of oyster sauce
1 teaspoon of sesame oil
½ head Chinese cabbage, roughly shredded
A large handful of bean sprouts

- Cook the noodles according to the instructions on the packet, drain and set aside.
- Heat a wok or a high-sided frying pan, until just before it begins smoking, stir fry the garlic and chilli in the sunflower oil for about 30 seconds.
- Add the shallots and fry for a further minute, and then add the carrot and shitake mushrooms, cooking for 3 minutes or until softened. Stir through the oyster sauce and sesame oil and cook for a further 2 minutes.
- Add the cabbage, bean sprouts and noodles to the pan, and toss well so all the ingredients are thoroughly combined. I like to add the cabbage and bean sprouts closer to the end so they keep their crunch, but if you want them to be cooked a little bit more add them at the same time as the mushrooms and carrots.
- Serve straightaway as a handy and quick Asian inspired dinner.

Crushed Herby Potatoes

This is a super side dish which goes really well with any main course.

Serves 4

Approximately 16 baby potatoes
1 bulb of garlic
A drizzle of olive oil
A good pinch of sea salt and ground black pepper
A handful of dill, roughly chopped
A handful of chives, chopped coarsely
A large handful of flat leaf parsley
2 tablespoons of extra virgin olive oil

- Before you start anything get the garlic in the oven. Cut off the top of the garlic so the tips of the cloves can just about be seen. Drizzle with a few drops of olive oil so the exposed tips are covered. Now cover in tinfoil and pop in the oven for 40 minutes at 200°C/400°F/Gas Mark 6.
- While the garlic is roasting, place the potatoes in a boiling pot of water and bring back to the boil. Simmer for 10–15 minutes or until the potatoes are tender – you can check this with a fork.
- While the potatoes are cooking prepare and chop your herbs. Drain the potatoes and tumble into a large mixing bowl. With a fork roughly crush each potato and season with salt and pepper.
- When the garlic is ready, pop out the cloves from their skins and mash with a fork on a chopping board. Transfer the garlic to the mixing bowl and add 2 tablespoons of extra virgin olive oil and scatter the dill, chives and parsley on top.
- Gently mix all the ingredients to combine, and be careful not to break up the potato too much.
- Serve in a large bowl with a final scattering of parsley and a drizzle of olive oil over the top.

Sesame Pasta Salad

Dishes packed with healthy ingredients and stunning colours are not only a cure for hunger, they can really improve your mood too. If you have a fridge full of leftover vegetables, this quick pasta salad is a great solution as you can transform the ingredients to your taste. I use a fairly basic mix of ingredients in this recipe but you can 'up the ante' by adding some pitted olives, or maybe even some garlic toasted croutons. It definitely beats any soggy mayonnaise-based pasta salads on sale in supermarkets.

Serves 2

250g/9oz wholewheat pasta
50g/2oz feta cheese, crumbled
1 red onion, sliced into half moons
1 carrot, finely chopped
½ small cucumber, finely chopped
2 tablespoons of olive oil
1 tablespoon of balsamic vinegar
A handful of basil, finely chopped
A handful of toasted sesame seeds
A good pinch of sea salt and black pepper

- Bring a large pot of water to the boil and add the pasta, cook until tender, then drain and set aside.
- While the pasta is cooking, prepare the vegetables, cheese and basil.
- In a large mixing bowl, add the oil and vinegar, and give it a quick whisk.
- Then add all the vegetables, cheese and herbs, and combine with the pasta.
- Give it a good pinch of salt and pepper, and serve. Top the finished dish with golden toasted sesame seeds.

Summer Salsa Salad

It can be so easy to produce healthy party food. Here's a great little finger salad for picking at parties. The salsa is contained in the baby gem lettuce leaves, making them easy to pick up and the perfect size for a hungry mouthful. If you're not afraid of a bit of heat, go ahead and stick in the whole chilli! This works great as a starter salad too.

Serves 2–4

1 red onion
1 mango
1 garlic clove, finely chopped
1 red pepper
2 baby gem lettuces, leaves separated and washed
½ cucumber, deseeded
½ red chilli, deseeded
1 large avocado
Juice of 1 small lime
A good pinch of sea salt and black pepper

- Chop the onion finely and add to a large mixing bowl.
- Slice the mango in three, avoiding the large flat stone in the centre; score the flesh on the two sides in a criss-cross pattern and push the skin inside out. You should now be able to cut the pre-sliced chunks straight off. Add the chunks to the bowl.
- Chop the garlic, red pepper, cucumber and chilli very finely, and add to the bowl.
- Cut the avocado in half, remove the stone and scoop out the flesh with a spoon. Chop roughly and add to the bowl. Mix through the juice of a lime to prevent the avocado discolouring.
- Combine all the ingredients well and season with salt and pepper.
- Arrange the leaves of the baby gem lettuces on a large serving plate.
- Add a large spoonful of the salsa on each leaf and serve straightaway.

Avocado and Lime Salsa

This little recipe is so basic anyone can do it. It requires absolutely no cooking and is essentially all preparation. I wasn't always a big fan of avocados and have only recently started eating them. But boy have I been missing out! These tasty little fruits are like a whole meal on their own and, packed with nutrients, they are a really powerful antioxidant food. This salsa is a brilliant way to serve avocados and even more perfect to munch with tortilla chips. Adjust the quantity of ingredients to your own taste. I like things hot, so use less Tabasco sauce if you want a milder mix.

Serves 4 as a snack

1 ripe avocado
Juice of 1 lime
½ red onion
1 teaspoon of Tabasco sauce
1 tablespoon of olive oil
A good pinch of sea salt and freshly ground pepper

- Cut the avocado lengthways and remove the stone.
- Scoop out the green flesh and chop finely, but don't worry too much as it all turns a bit mushy when you add the rest of the ingredients.
- Add a squeeze of lime juice to stop it discolouring and add to a medium-sized bowl.
- Chop the red onion finely and add to the avocado.
- Mix together the rest of the ingredients with the onion and avocado to your desired consistency and that's it. Enjoy!

Tahini Noodle Toss

This little recipe came about after I ate at the California Pizza Kitchen in America; they served a really tasty crisp salad, with this rich and tasty peanut dressing. I recreated it from taste, adapted it and recently discovered it goes perfectly with noodles. This is another great little lunch box filler as it can be served hot and cold. Tahini is a creamy, yet smoky paste made from sesame seeds and is similar to peanut butter, which you can also use as a substitute. I sometimes add finely shredded raw Chinese cabbage to these noodles for extra crunch. I love this recipe because you basically combine all the wet and dry ingredients just before serving.

250g/9oz wholewheat noodles
4 spring onions, finely sliced
1 large garlic clove, finely chopped
1 chilli, deseeded and finely chopped
4 tablespoons of tahini paste
1 tablespoon of sunflower oil
1 tablespoon of soy sauce

1 tablespoon of oyster sauce
1 tablespoon of rice wine vinegar
1 teaspoon of sesame oil
A good handful of bean sprouts
Toasted sesame seeds
A small handful of coriander, freshly
   chopped

Serves 2

- Cook the noodles according to the instructions on the packet, rinse in cold water and set aside.
- In a small saucepan, fry the garlic and chilli for about 30 seconds, then add the soy sauce, oyster sauce, rice wine vinegar, sesame oil and tahini paste.
- Cook over a medium heat until the mixture comes to the boil and, when it does, reduce the heat and simmer for 3 minutes.
- In a large mixing bowl, add the noodles and bean sprouts, toss together with the tahini sauce until mixed through.
- Serve in hearty bowls and top with toasted sesame seeds, freshly chopped coriander and thinly sliced spring onions. Time to get those chopsticks out!

Hasselback Potatoes

I came across the recipe for Hasselback potatoes when I was younger and they are so visually appealing that I had to make them. The traditional recipe, originally from Stockholm, calls for breadcrumbs and cheese, but I have tried to make it as simple as possible for this recipe. The potatoes go nicely alongside most dishes. If your potato slices don't separate while cooking, increase your heat and you should get better results.

Serves 4

Approximately 20 baby potatoes
2 tablespoons of melted butter
A generous pinch of sea salt

- These potatoes are a little bit daunting at first, but once you get the knack of it you'll have no trouble! The idea is to cut slices about 3mm in thickness right across the potato, but to keep them attached at the bottom.
- If that all sounds a bit too much, there is a quick trick you can use: place the potatoes on a wooden spoon and slice down: the dip in the spoon will prevent you from slicing all the way through.
- When you're finished, place all the potatoes sliced side up in a roasting tray and brush each one with the melted butter and give a good sprinkling of coarse sea salt.
- Roast at 200°C/400°F/Gas Mark 6 for approximately 45 minutes or until the slices of the potatoes fan out and turn golden brown.
- Serve straightaway and dig in!

Smoked Salmon and Dill Sandwich

This recipe always reminds me of working at a Christmas smorgasbord restaurant in Gothenburg, Sweden, where we churned out traditional Swedish food by the lorry-load! The most popular dish was always hard-boiled eggs, topped with mayonnaise, prawns, fish roe and a sprinkle of dill. I could hardly produce these little babies quick enough to keep up with the amount of trays the diners used to eat. They were like gold dust! This is my Irish answer to the Swedish dish, and is a regular for my homesick Swedish girlfriend. Use eggs which are close to their best before date, as fresh eggs can be extremely difficult to peel.

Serves 4

250g/9oz pre-sliced smoked salmon
4 large free range eggs
3 tablespoons of chopped chives
A little softened butter
8 slices of brown soda bread
A squeeze of lemon juice
A good handful of fresh dill, chopped coarsely
A pinch of salt and pepper

- Place the eggs in a pot and cover with water. Bring the pot to the boil and continue to cook at a steady simmer for 4–5 minutes. Take the pot off the heat, drain the hot water and fill with cold water. Allow the eggs to sit in the cold water until cool.
- With a fork, combine the butter and chives, and spread a thin layer over the slices of bread. Top with a generous amount of smoked salmon and add a good squeeze of lemon juice.
- Peel the shell from the eggs and cut into ½cm slices; the yolk should still be a little soft. Place the egg slices on top of the salmon and garnish with a sprinkling of dill and a pinch of salt and pepper.
- Serve straightaway.

Broad Bean, Pancetta and Pea Shoot Salad

I have a bit of an obsession with pea shoots, and have to stop myself nibbling on them when they're in the kitchen. It used to be quite hard to get your hands on these tasty little greens, but it's becoming more and more common to see them in local supermarkets, which is really great. They go really well with this zingin' little dressing too! If you can't manage to get pea shoots, substitute them with any other shoots for this recipe.

Serves 4

200g/7oz pancetta, cut into pieces, or bacon bits
450g/1lb frozen broad beans, defrosted
1 large garlic clove
Juice of ½ lime
1 tablespoon of honey
3 tablespoons of extra virgin olive oil
1 teaspoon of Dijon mustard
4 large handfuls of rocket
A good handful of pea shoots per person
A good chunk of parmesan cheese
A good pinch of sea salt

- Heat a large frying pan and fry the pancetta pieces for about 5 minutes until crispy. You shouldn't need any oil as the pancetta should render its own fat. Remove from the heat and place on a plate on a piece of kitchen paper.
- Crush the garlic clove with the back of a knife, remove the skin, and add a tiny bit of sea salt and continue to crush with the back of the knife until a smooth paste forms.
- In the bottom of a large salad bowl, combine the mashed garlic, lime juice, honey, olive oil and Dijon mustard. Add in the broad beans, rocket and pea shoots. Toss until everything is combined.
- With a peeler, shave wafer thin slices of parmesan cheese over the salad and serve straightaway.

Nacha's Toasted Pumpkin Seeds

We always had two massive pumpkins every Halloween, when my brother and I were growing up. Carving pumpkins became an annual tradition and everyone had a role. My brother and I would draw the faces, my mom would gut the pumpkins, and my dad would carve them. There were always huge arguments over choosing the right pumpkin and even more competition when it came to drawing the best and most scary face! I picked up this recipe from our first au-pair from France, Nacha, who taught us never to throw away any of the precious seeds. They are so tasty toasted with butter and sea salt. Here's the simple recipe.

The seeds of 2 large pumpkins
4 tablespoons of melted butter
A generous pinch of coarse sea salt and ground black pepper

- Cut off the top of the pumpkins. Using your hands, separate the seeds from the flesh and transfer to a colander.
- Rinse the seeds under cold water and pick out any remaining stringy orange flesh. Transfer to a few sheets of kitchen paper or a dry tea towel and pat dry.
- Tip the seeds into a large roasting dish and spoon over the melted butter. Toss the seeds so they are all coated in the butter and season with sea salt and black pepper.
- Toast in the oven at 200°C/390°F/Gas Mark 6, for 20 minutes or until nice and golden.

Houmous with a Kick

This is another really simple party snack, which you can produce in minutes. Plus your guests will think you went to a whole lot of trouble. The things you can get away with when you have a few foodie tricks up your sleeve! I will warn you though – this *really* is houmous with a kick, so if you're not a spice fiend like me, ease off on the cayenne pepper.

Serves 4–6

400g tin chickpeas, drained and rinsed
2 garlic cloves, crushed
4 tablespoons of extra virgin olive oil
1 teaspoon of freshly ground cumin
1 tablespoon of tahini paste
1 teaspoon of cayenne pepper
Juice of ½ lemon
A good pinch of sea salt

- Pour the chickpeas into a food processor and add the garlic cloves, olive oil, cumin, tahini paste, lemon juice, cayenne pepper and sea salt.
- Blitz until smooth, and if your mixture looks a little too stiff, simply loosen it with a little water.
- Drizzle a little extra olive oil over it and serve with some crudités, toast or toasted wholemeal pitta pockets, then dig in!
- The houmous will last covered in a fridge for 4–5 days.

Nut Snack Mix

Most supermarkets carry their own range of nuts in little plastic packets, which are perfect for this recipe. Completely addictive and so simple to make, you won't even notice you're getting your daily dose of nutty health benefits.

Makes a 200g mix

50g/2oz almonds
50g/2oz walnuts
50g/2oz pinenuts
50g/2oz sunflower seeds
2 tablespoons of olive oil
2 teaspoons of dried oregano
2 sprigs of fresh thyme, chopped
2 teaspoons of freshly chopped rosemary
A good pinch of cayenne pepper
A good pinch of coarse sea salt and ground black pepper

- In a large roasting tray combine the almonds, walnuts, pine nuts and sunflower seeds.
- Add the oil, cayenne pepper, oregano, thyme, rosemary, black pepper, salt, and mix through so that all the nuts are coated. There are so many flavour combinations that you can play around with here. Try adding other spices like ground cumin and cinnamon to find your favourite mix.
- Roast the nuts in the oven for 35–45 minutes at 180°C/350°F/Gas Mark 4, and make sure to give them a good toss halfway through the cooking time. Keep an eye on them – nuts can burn very easily!
- Serve as a great little party snack, or blitz for a few seconds in a blender as a crunchy salad topping.

Warm Cherry Tomato Bruschetta

Apologies in advance to those who may find it slightly sacrilegious to heat the tomatoes for a bruschetta, and I'm sure there are Italians out there who may crucify me over this recipe, but this is the way I like to do it.

Makes 4 bruschetta

1 punnet of cherry tomatoes
1 garlic clove
A good glug of extra virgin olive oil
A handful of fresh basil, finely chopped
Some nice hearty Italian bread like ciabatta or focaccia
A good pinch of sea salt and ground black pepper

- This is a quick one: smash some garlic under a knife to quickly get rid of the skin, then finely chop it. In a pan heat the oil and fry the garlic for 30 seconds.
- Throw in the tomatoes and toss well with the garlic. Turn down the heat and leave to soften for 5 minutes.
- In the meantime, cut the bread into rough slices and toast them.
- Remove the tomatoes from the heat. With a fork gently squash them down, mix in the basil and spread the mix on the toast.
- Serve with a good pinch of sea salt and black pepper.

Chilli Jam

Enjoy this spicy, sweet jam with sandwiches, alongside meat or fish dishes, or as a delicious dipping sauce.

Makes approximately 1 litre of jam

1kg/2½lbs tomatoes (I used approximately 16 tomatoes)
3 medium red chillies, deseeded and roughly chopped
4 garlic cloves, crushed
2 thumb-sized pieces of ginger, peeled and roughly chopped
2 tablespoons of Thai fish sauce (Nam Pla)
450g/1lb Demerara sugar
100ml/4fl oz red wine vinegar
1 tablespoon of balsamic vinegar

- Place half the tomatoes into a food processor and blitz until finely chopped. Transfer to a medium saucepan.
- Place the rest of the tomatoes, red chillies, garlic, ginger and Thai fish sauce into the food processor and blitz until it becomes a smooth paste. Transfer to the pan and place over a medium heat.
- Stir through the sugar, balsamic vinegar and red wine vinegar. Bring to the boil stirring regularly, then reduce the heat and keep at a steady simmer for 35 minutes or until the jam has reduced by half its volume. Stir every 5 minutes.
- When the jam has cooked allow to cool and then transfer to sterilised jars. Cover and place in the fridge.
- This recipe makes approximately 1 litre/2 pints of jam; I distributed this amongst a variety of jars. You can check what fits by filling them beforehand with 1 litre/2 pints of water from a measuring jug.
- If you don't plan on using all the jam at once, you will need to sterilise the jars you use in order for the jam to last longer.
- To sterilise the jars and lids wash with boiling water, rinse and dry in an oven for 5–10 minutes on a baking tray at 150°C/300°F/Gas Mark 2. Be careful, the glass gets quite hot.

Homemade Spicy Tomato Ketchup

I'll level with you; sometimes you just can't do without a good blob of ketchup on some meals. But there is nothing better than making your own. You can make this to use straightaway, but if you wash a couple of old jars and bang them in a moderate oven for a few minutes to sterilise them, you can pour in the ketchup and it should keep in the fridge for much longer.

Makes 2 generous jars

2 x 400g tins plum tomatoes
2 garlic cloves, finely chopped
1 onion, finely chopped
2 tablespoons of olive oil
2 tablespoons of balsamic vinegar
1 teaspoon of cinnamon
1 teaspoon of ground coriander seeds
1 teaspoon of dried mustard powder
2 tablespoons of brown sugar
½ teaspoon of chilli powder
Sea salt and freshly ground pepper

- Fry the garlic and onion in the olive oil in a large frying pan over a high heat for 2 minutes, add the balsamic vinegar and cook for a further minute.
- Add the cinnamon, ground coriander seeds, mustard powder, brown sugar and chilli powder. Stir through and cook for another minute. Add the tomatoes and mix, breaking them up with a fork.
- Bring to a steady simmer and cook for 15–20 minutes, making sure to stir every few minutes so it does not burn at the bottom.
- Season the sauce with salt and pepper, take the pan off the heat and allow to cool. In a food processor, blend until smooth, and decant into sterilised jars and store in the fridge.

Calming and Nutritious Dinners

Calming and Nutritious Dinners

Dinnertime is the one real chance in a day that you get to sit down and relax with your food.

The food we eat before bedtime can really affect sleeping patterns, and choosing more calming foods and eating at a regular time each evening can create a very solid routine.

Allow time for your body to digest the food you eat in the evening. Going to sleep directly after eating means your body will most likely still be digesting food and won't be ready for sleep, which can lead to a restless night.

Eating wholesome foods throughout the day means you can easily manage a smaller meal in the evening, and you won't be starving by the end of the day.

After a long day at work it can be quite daunting having to conjure up meals in minutes. With this in mind, I have included some really easy and tasty recipes which will allow you not only to enjoy the cooking, but more importantly, the eating!

If you do have time, many of the recipes here are also perfect for entertaining, so don't be afraid to double the ingredients or adapt the recipes if you need to cook for a larger group. Also many of the recipes can be made ahead of time, so get into the habit of preparing things the night before, it takes a matter of minutes and it will make feeding big numbers a lot more manageable and far less stressful.

Tasty Chicken Drumstick Stew

This is my ultimate one pot wonder dish! There is nothing better than a big hearty pot of stew, plonked on the table with a ladle, when it's cold outside. I use chicken drumsticks here, but lamb shanks or any cheap cut of meat also works really well in this dish. You can also bump up the veggies here by adding leeks or a few stalks of celery.

Serves 4

10 free range chicken drumsticks
2 x 400g tins chopped tomatoes
100ml/4fl oz chicken stock
100ml/4fl oz red wine
4 medium carrots, chopped into chunks
2 red peppers, coarsely chopped
6 garlic cloves, crushed
2 red onions, peeled and quartered

3 teaspoons of dried oregano
4 sprigs of rosemary
2 tablespoons of honey
2 tablespoons of sunflower oil
2 teaspoons of English mustard powder
Juice of 1 lemon
A good pinch of sea salt and black pepper

- Heat a large cast iron ovenproof casserole dish on the hob, add 1 tablespoon of oil and brown the chicken drumsticks on all sides.
- Remove the drumsticks from the casserole dish and set aside.
- Fry the garlic, onions, oregano and rosemary in 1 tablespoon of oil for 2 minutes.
- Add the carrots and peppers and fry for a further 2 minutes. Place the drumsticks back in the pot and pour over the wine, chicken stock, lemon juice, honey and chopped tomatoes.
- Season with salt, pepper and mustard powder. Cover and place in the oven at 220°C/425°F/Gas Mark 7 for 45 minutes or until the chicken is cooked through.
- Serve as a hearty winter warming dinner with a big chunk of crusty bread to mop up any leftover juices.

Herby Roast Chicken

I'm very proud of this roast chicken recipe; it really gives an intense and deep herb flavour to the bird. Roast chicken was a classic dish while we were growing up, we ate it practically every Sunday without fail! This recipe calls for lemon balm, but unless you are growing it in your garden, it's not so easy to come across as an ingredient. You can replace it here with half a lemon, which will still give a fragrant citrus flavour to the chicken. As I mentioned in the section on growing your own herbs, lemon balm is a really easy herb to grow. Keep it in its own pot, water regularly and snip off the fresh sprigs when needed; it should last you a long time.

Serves 4–6

1 free range chicken
A generous handful of lemon balm (or half a lemon)
2 large sprigs of rosemary
3 sprigs of thyme
2 garlic cloves
A small handful of fresh basil, finely chopped
A small handful parsley, finely chopped
1 teaspoon of dried oregano
A good pinch of sea salt and freshly ground pepper
2 tablespoons of olive oil

149

- Place the chicken in a large roasting tin. Stuff the cavity evenly with the lemon balm (or lemon half), rosemary and thyme. In a pestle and mortar, smash the garlic, basil, parsley and dried oregano with the salt and pepper.
- Add the olive oil and mix thoroughly so you have a thick herby paste. Spread the paste all over the chicken, paying special attention to the breasts, where you can push the mixture under the skin.
- Roast in the oven at 220°C/425°F/Gas Mark 7 for 1¼–1½ hours (depending on the size of the chicken, smaller chickens will need less time), or until the juices run clear when poked with a skewer.
- Serve with a good selection of roast vegetables or a nice green salad.

Perfect Parsnips

Try to select interesting-shaped parsnips, they look great when they're roasted. I try and cut the parsnips as thin as possible because when they roast in the oven you should end up with thick fleshy tops and tasty crispy ends.

Makes enough for 4 side dishes

1kg/2½lbs parsnips
3 tablespoons of wholemeal flour
1 tablespoon of ground black pepper
1 tablespoon of sea salt
2 tablespoons of olive oil
A generous handful of parmesan cheese

- Preheat the oven to 200°C/400°F/Gas Mark 6.
- Peel the parsnips and chop in half and then slice into four. You may need to slice the chunks in half again depending on what size you want them.
- Place the parsnips in a pot and cover with cold water. Bring the pot to the boil and simmer for 4 minutes. Rinse with a little cold water and drain the chunks in a colander.
- Combine the flour, pepper and salt in a large bowl.
- Tumble the parsnips into the bowl and toss to coat. Place in a large roasting tray, sprinkle over the parmesan cheese and drizzle with olive oil.
- Roast in the oven for 25 minutes or until golden brown and crispy.

Asian Steam Baked Fish Parcels

Making this dish is just about as satisfying as eating it. The fish are steam baked in their own little tinfoil parcels, so make sure to lay out lots of tinfoil – there is nothing worse then a leaky steam bake parcel! You can bake the fish whole, or ask your fishmonger to fillet it for you. This dish is perfect for alfresco eating and the tinfoil parcels are also great cooked on the barby.

Serves 4

4 small seabass or 8 seabass fillets	4 tablespoons of soy sauce
4 bok choy or pak choy	4 teaspoons of sesame oil
4 large cloves of garlic	4 tablespoons of rice wine vinegar
4 small leeks	Juice of 2 limes
2 red chillis	Sesame seeds
2 thumb-sized pieces of ginger	Coarsely chopped coriander to garnish
1 large bunch of spring onions	(optional)

- You will need 4 large sheets of tinfoil. The main body of work in this recipe is in the preparation rather than the actual cooking. To begin, prepare the ginger, garlic and chilli. Chop both the chilli and garlic finely. Peel the ginger and cut into fine strips. Slice the spring onions into delicate, thin slices on the diagonal and set aside. Prepare the bok choy and leeks by cutting right down the centre.

- To create the fish parcels, simply lay the bok choy and leeks in the centre of the tinfoil and place the seabass fillets on top.

- Sprinkle generously with the ginger slices, finely chopped garlic and chilli, and top with sesame seeds. Bring two opposite sides of the foil together creating a small tent, then fold tightly together to form a seal. Seal one of the open ends by making three small folds towards the centre.

- In the open end pour combined soy sauce, rice wine vinegar, lime juice and sesame oil. Repeat this process with the other fillets.

- Bake in the oven for 15–20 minutes at 200°C/400°F/Gas Mark 6 (if using whole seabass bake for 25–30 minutes) and serve in the foil, opening the parcels to release the fragrant aromas. Top with a generous sprinkle of chopped coriander.

Chicken Thigh Supper

This is a super dish for a big group of people, served with a tasty salad; it's perfect for weekday entertaining. If you can't get a hold of chicken thighs, you can use any other cuts as long as they're on the bone. This gives the meat a really great flavour.

Serves 4

6–8 chicken thighs
200g pancetta, diced, or bacon bits
1 x 400g tin chopped tomatoes
75ml/3fl oz red wine
2 garlic cloves, sliced thinly
1 red onion, chopped in half moons
2 sprigs of rosemary
2 sprigs of thyme
2 teaspoons of English mustard powder
2 tablespoons of olive oil

- In a large deep frying pan, heat 1 tablespoon of olive oil, and brown the chicken and pancetta, until you get a nice colour on the thighs. Set aside on plate covered with kitchen paper.
- In the same pan, add the rest of the oil and fry the garlic, onion, rosemary and thyme for 2 minutes. Sprinkle over the mustard powder and stir through.
- Add the tinned tomatoes and red wine, and bring to the boil. Add the chicken and pancetta pieces back to the pan, turning the chicken pieces to coat.
- Cover the pan and cook for 20 minutes over a low heat or until the chicken is cooked through. You may need to extend the cooking time depending on the size of the chicken thighs. I don't add salt to this recipe as the pancetta can be quite salty, but make sure to taste it and add seasoning if needed.
- Serve with a tasty salad and some hearty wholemeal bread.

Open Aromatic Duck Salad

This is basically an adaptation of the classic aromatic duck and pancake dish which is available at most Chinese restaurants. It's one of my favourite dishes and is so simple to produce. The tender crispy duck goes well with the fresh raw vegetables and tangy Asian dressing.

Serves 2

1 crispy half duck portion (available pre-cooked at most supermarkets)
2 large carrots, thinly sliced
½ cucumber, thinly sliced
½ Chinese cabbage, finely shredded
Bunch of spring onions, thinly sliced

For the dressing:
Juice of ½ lime
2 garlic cloves, finely chopped
1 thumb-sized piece of ginger, peeled and finely chopped
2 tablespoons of rice wine vinegar
2 tablespoons of oyster sauce
1 teaspoon of sesame oil

- Before you start, put the duck in a roasting tin (you can stick the breast on a wire wrack, this way the fat will drip) and place in the oven for approximately 20 minutes at 200°C/400°F/Gas Mark 6 or until heated through.
- In a large mixing bowl mix the ingredients for the dressing. Add the carrot, cucumber, cabbage and spring onions, and toss to combine.
- Take the duck out of the oven, slice thinly and add to the salad. Serve straightaway.

Our Family Stew

This is a really tasty one-pot dinner which is perfect for cold winter evenings. Ask your butcher for stewing steak, which is normally available, but you can also use any other cheap cuts of meat. You will need a large casserole dish.

Serves 6 people

700g/1½lbs stewing steak
1½ litres/3 pints beef stock
5 large potatoes peeled and sliced into 1cm discs
4 large carrots, chopped roughly
2 large onions, chopped in quarters
3 tablespoons of wholemeal flour
3 teaspoons of ground black pepper
2 tablespoons of sunflower oil
2 bay leaves
A good pinch of sea salt
A good handful of freshly chopped parsley

- Preheat the oven to 200°C/400°F/Gas Mark 6.
- Place the stewing steak, wholemeal flour, and black pepper in a resealable plastic bag. Seal the bag and give it a good shake so that all the steak pieces have a nice coating of flour and pepper.
- Heat a tablespoon of sunflower oil in a large frying pan and brown half the steak pieces. Transfer the steak pieces to the casserole dish. Repeat with the rest of the meat.
- Fry the onions in the meat juices in the pan for 2 minutes, adding an extra drop of oil if necessary. Transfer the onions to the casserole dish.
- Add the carrots, beef stock, sea salt and bay leaves to the casserole dish, and stir through. Add the potato slices on top, season with a generous amount of black pepper and cover with the lid.
- Transfer the casserole dish to the oven and cook for 1½ hours.
- Serve straight from the casserole dish to some large bowls with some tasty wholemeal bread. Sprinkle the parsley on top and enjoy!

Zingy Courgette Fritters

These are really tasty little fritters that are light and refreshing and go perfectly with tzatziki (p.99). They are also great finger food and can be served with any tasty dipping sauce.

Makes 10–12 fritters

2 courgettes, chopped into fine chunks
3 carrots, grated
2 eggs
1 red onion, finely chopped
50g/2oz feta cheese
Zest of 1 lemon
A large handful of mint and dill, finely chopped
1 tablespoon of olive oil
1 tablespoon of extra virgin olive oil
A pinch of sea salt and a pinch of cayenne pepper

- Sauté the onion in a little olive oil until soft, then add the courgette and cook for 5–6 minutes or until soft. Stir through the grated carrot and cook for a further two minutes and set aside.
- Take out two mixing bowls, one large and one medium-sized. Separate the eggs, add the yolk to the large bowl and keep the whites in the other.
- Whisk the yolks with the lemon zest, mint, dill, salt and cayenne pepper.
- Add the courgette mixture to the yolks and mix through. Crumble the feta cheese on top and mix through.
- In the other bowl, with a clean whisk, beat the eggs whites until soft peaks form, and fold into the courgette mixture.
- In a large frying pan, heat 1 tablespoon of extra virgin olive oil over a low to medium heat, and dollop dessertspoons of the mixture onto the pan. Make sure to keep your fritters small because if they are too big you will end up with a courgette omelette when you go to turn them.
- Cook for 2–3 minutes on either side or until golden brown. Serve with a crunchy side salad and top with a mix of alfalfa and brocco shoots.

Steaks in Chimichurri

Chimichurri is a really tasty little herb paste perfect for grilled meats and oozing with flavour. The sauce is originally from Argentina and you can now pick up the marinade fairly easily in supermarkets, but it's so simple to make yourself with just a couple of simple store-cupboard ingredients. When you're selecting your steaks try and look out for ones with an even marbling of fat and a rich red colour.

Serves 4

4 large striploin steaks
1 medium onion, finely chopped
4 garlic cloves, chopped
2 handfuls of fresh parsley, chopped
1 teaspoon of dried oregano
6 tablespoons of extra virgin olive oil
3 tablespoons of red wine vinegar
A pinch of cayenne pepper and sea salt

- Combine the parsley, oregano, garlic, cayenne pepper, sea salt and onion in a pestle and mortar and pound until it forms a paste. Loosen the paste by adding the extra virgin olive oil and red wine vinegar.
- Place the steaks on a plate and smother with the Chimichurri sauce, cover with cling film and let them sit in the fridge for at least 30 minutes.
- Heat a griddle pan until just before it begins smoking, add the steak and griddle for 2–3 minutes either side for medium and a little longer if you prefer a more well-done steak.
- Remove from the pan and allow the meat to rest for at least 2–3 minutes.
- Serve with a crispy baked potato and some steamed greens, or slice thinly and pack into a crusty roll with some salad leaves and Dijon mustard.

Roast Sweet Potato and Parsnip Mash

This is a super accompaniment to any meal. The combination of the two vegetables creates a really wonderful taste.

Serves 4

2 large sweet potatoes
2 medium parsnips
2 teaspoons of butter
A pinch of ground cumin
A pinch of sea salt and pepper
A handful of coarsely chopped parsley

- Preheat the oven to 200°C/400°F/Gas Mark 6.
- Place the two sweet potatoes into a roasting tray and place in the oven for about 30 minutes.
- Meanwhile, peel the parsnips and chop into rough chunks and place in a pot of boiling water. Bring the pot back to the boil and simmer for 10–15 minutes or until tender. Drain the water and mash with a potato masher.
- When the sweet potatoes are cooked they should be nice and mushy. Slice them in half lengthways, scoop out the flesh with a spoon and mix with the parsnips.
- Add the butter, cumin, salt, pepper and parsley, and mix through.
- Serve straightaway with an extra sprinkle of parsley.

Goat's Cheese and Broccoli Pasta

I came up with this recipe, tired and in need of a big bowl of warmth, and it provides just that! This is a really enjoyable, hassle-free dinner, which can be cooked in a matter of minutes. I have also tried this with asparagus instead of broccoli and it works just as well.

Serves 2

225g/8oz wholewheat pasta
100g/4oz goat's cheese
1 head of broccoli, approximately 200g/7oz
1 large garlic clove, finely chopped
2 tablespoons of freshly chopped parsley
Sea salt and freshly ground pepper

- Cook the pasta as directed in salted water. Cut the broccoli into florets and steam for approximately 5 minutes or until tender.
- While the pasta and broccoli are cooking, mince the garlic, chop with fresh parsley and add to a large bowl.
- When the broccoli is cooked chop it finely on a chopping board and add to the bowl.
- When the pasta is cooked, tumble the hot pasta into the bowl and crumble the goat's cheese over it.
- Stir the cheese through so you get a nice coating all over the pasta.
- Season the mix with a little sea salt and freshly ground pepper. Serve straightaway.
- This also makes a great little lunch box filler, so I normally make more than enough for an extra portion.

Cajun Salmon

This has to be my number one favourite way to enjoy salmon fillets — a spicy crust concealing tender pink flesh, makes for a very tasty mouthful. Salmon has long been one of the original superfoods of the fish world, as it is rich in Omega 3. Great for healthy joints.

Serves 2

2 salmon fillets
1 teaspoon of white pepper
1 teaspoon of garlic powder
1 teaspoon of onion powder
1 teaspoon of cayenne pepper
1 teaspoon of paprika
1 teaspoon of black pepper

- Mix the spices for the topping together and lay out in a thin layer on a large plate.
- Place the salmon fillets flesh side down pressing to ensure a good coating of seasoning. Place under a hot grill and cook for approximately 7–8 minutes.
- The salmon changes to a lighter shade of pink when it is cooked. Serve with steamed veggies for a really tasty dish.

Basil and Sweetcorn

I picked this recipe up while staying with my lovely Auntie Annie in Florida, and it's a real discovery. The combination of basil and sweetcorn works together to create a really interesting taste and a perfect side dish to grilled meat or chicken. The recipe itself is fairly straightforward and definitely worth trying.

Serves 4

4 cooked corn-on-the-cob
A good handful of fresh basil
1 tablespoon of butter
A good sprinkle of salt and pepper

- In a large bowl, slice the corn off the cob. Chop the basil roughly and put to the side.
- Place a saucepan over a medium heat and add the butter until melted.
- Add the corn, toss, and then add the basil. Keep the mixture moving by stirring for about 3 minutes.
- Season with the salt and pepper and serve piping hot!

Herby Roast Baby Potatoes and Roast Garlic

This recipe always has my mouth watering at the thought of it. The process takes the pungent garlic cloves and transforms them into a smoky, sweet and wonderfully creamy mush.

Serves 4

16–20 baby potatoes
1 whole garlic bulb with the top sliced off
1 tablespoon of balsamic vinegar
1 tablespoon of olive oil
3 large sprigs of fresh rosemary
A large handful of fresh sage leaves
A small handful of thyme
Sea salt and freshly ground pepper

- Put the potatoes and whole garlic bulb in a large roasting tray, and coat with the salt, pepper, balsamic vinegar and olive oil.
- Remove the leaves from the rosemary sprigs and roughly chop with the sage and thyme. Scatter the herbs over the potatoes and garlic, and toss together.
- Roast in the oven for about 45 minutes at 200°C/400°F/Gas Mark 6, or until the potatoes are cooked.
- When cooked, squeeze out the soft garlic cloves into the roasting tray, and with the back of a fork mash the cloves. Make sure to incorporate any of the leftover oils and herbs in the bottom of the tray.
- Scoop up the garlic mush and distribute over the potatoes. Give a good toss and serve straightaway.

Pear, Parmesan and Bacon Salad

Rocket and parmesan cheese are a match made in food heaven: the pepperiness of rocket and sweet nuttiness of a good parmesan make the base for this tasty salad. I griddle the pears and nuts in this recipe, but if you are stuck for time, simply slice the pears thinly and throw in the nuts as is, and it should be just as tasty. If you can't find pancetta, a packet of bacon bits are the perfect substitute or even a few slices of good bacon from the butcher.

Serves 4

4 pears, quartered and pips removed
4 large handfuls of rocket
150g/5oz pancetta, cut roughly into chunks, or bacon bits
2 tablespoons of balsamic vinegar
4 tablespoons of olive oil
2 handfuls of parmesan cheese shavings
A small handful of pine nuts
A small handful of walnuts, lightly crushed

- Give the rocket leaves a good rinse and spin dry, place in a large salad bowl and set aside.
- Heat a large griddle pan until just before it starts smoking, add the pancetta and cook until nice and crispy, then set aside on a piece of kitchen paper.
- Place the pear quarters on one side of the pan and nuts on the other.
- Dribble 1 tablespoon of balsamic vinegar over the pears as they cook, and turn them when they have a nice golden colour and some great sear marks on their flesh from the griddle pan.
- Toss the nuts until golden brown, this will really bring out their flavour.
- Remove the pears and the nuts from the pan and set alongside the pancetta.
- Combine the olive oil and the rest of the balsamic vinegar, and dress the rocket leaves with the mix. Serve topped with the pears, nuts and a generous handful of parmesan shavings.

My Healthy Paella

When I discovered this dish, I drove everyone mad by cooking it every chance I got. In this recipe I'm using brown basmati rice which is unrefined and retains much more nutrition than its refined version. This recipe is very adaptable and I have made it with different vegetables, and with and without the prawns, so make it to your taste. The quickest way of cooking this dish is to prepare everything beforehand; that way things move a little more smoothly and it also prevents any stopping and starting.

Serves 4

2 chicken breasts
120g/4oz fresh, peeled prawns (or use good quality frozen, defrosted)
300g/11oz chorizo sausage, cut into chunky slices
1 x 400g tin chopped tomatoes
170g/6oz brown basmati rice
400ml/14fl oz chicken stock
1 red pepper, finely chopped

1 small squash, peeled and chopped into small pieces
2 garlic cloves, finely chopped
2 tablespoons of olive oil
A handful of fresh parsley chopped
A generous pinch of paprika
A pinch of sea salt and ground black pepper
A good squeeze of lemon juice to serve

- In a small bowl marinate the prawns in half the finely chopped garlic, 1 tablespoon of olive oil, paprika and black pepper.
- Fry the chorizo in a pan without oil – the fat from the sausage should be enough to prevent any sticking. When the chorizo is flaming red and sizzling remove from the pan and set aside on a dish lined with a paper towel.
- Slice the chicken breasts thinly and fry off in the chorizo oil with black pepper to season. Remove the slices from the pan and set aside with the cooked chorizo.
- In the same pan, fry off the remaining garlic and red pepper in a tablespoon of olive oil until golden. Then add the squash and tomatoes and cook until soft. Add the rice, coating well with the contents of the pan. Add the stock and salt, and bring to a steady simmer for 15 minutes. Finally add the fresh prawns, chorizo and chicken and simmer for a final five minutes.
- Serve in a large bowl with a scattering of freshly chopped parsley and a good squeeze of a lemon.

Oven Roasted Sausage and Sweet Potato

Try and get your hands on some really thick and interesting sausages for this recipe, it will make the whole dish come alive! Your local butcher should have a good selection – ask for sausages with 80 per cent meat. This is perfect for a quick all-in-one tray dinner, just prepare everything ahead of time, bang it in the oven, leave it to roast and dinner is served!

Serves 4

8 large, good quality sausages
4 sweet potatoes, chopped into chunks
2 large carrots, peeled and chopped into chunks
3 red onions, peeled and quartered
1 garlic bulb with the top sliced off
75ml/3fl oz red wine
1 tablespoon of English mustard powder
2 teaspoons of dried oregano
1 tablespoon of honey
A small handful of sage leaves

- Arrange the sweet potatoes in a roasting tin with the sausages, whole garlic bulb, carrots and red onion.
- Give the tray a good slosh of red wine, sprinkle with the mustard powder, sage leaves and oregano, and drizzle with the honey.
- Give the tray a good toss in order to coat all the vegetables and the sausages. Make sure not to overload the tray.
- Put in an oven at 220°C/425°F/Gas Mark 7 for approximately 50–55 minutes.
- Serve straight from the roasting tray. Make sure to spoon over any remaining juices.

Teriyaki Salmon with Sesame Noodles

Salmon is an extremely healthy ingredient to cook with. If you have any leftovers, this tasty sauce can also be used tossed through a crunchy Asian salad.

Makes 2 portions

2 salmon fillets skinned
3 tablespoons of teriyaki sauce
150g/5oz egg noodles
1 red chilli, deseeded and finely chopped
3 garlic cloves, finely chopped
1 tablespoon of dark brown sugar
5 tablespoons of soy sauce
2 tablespoons of sunflower oil
2 teaspoons of sesame oil
A small handful of toasted sesame seeds
Juice and zest of 1 lime

- Slice the salmon into bite-sized chunks and place in a bowl with the teriyaki sauce. Cover and place in the fridge to marinate. While the salmon is marinating prepare the rest of the ingredients.
- Cook the noodles according to instructions on the packet, drain and toss with a teaspoon of sesame oil and the sesame seeds.
- In a small saucepan fry the chilli and garlic in 1 tablespoon of sunflower oil over for approximately 2 minutes.
- Add the brown sugar, soy sauce, lime juice, zest and the 1 teaspoon of sesame oil, and bring to the boil, then reduce the heat and allow the sauce to bubble away gently for about 6–8 minutes.
- While the sauce is cooking, in a large frying pan fry the salmon pieces in 1 tablespoon of sunflower oil over a medium heat until browned on all sides.
- Serve the salmon pieces on top of the noodles and drizzle over the sauce.

Steak and Mushroom Pie

Makes 6 mini pies or 1 large pie

700g/1½lbs stewing steak or diced beef

500ml/16fl oz beef stock

250g/9oz mushrooms, finely sliced

250g/9oz ready to roll puff pastry

2 egg yolks

4 garlic cloves, finely chopped

2 red onions, finely chopped

4 tablespoons of wholemeal flour

2 tablespoons of sunflower oil

A generous pinch of sea salt and ground black pepper

- Toss the meat pieces in a little wholemeal flour. Heat a tablespoon of oil in a large frying pan, and brown the meat on all sides. You may need to fry the meat in batches in order to get a nice colour. Remove from the pan and set aside. Add the rest of the oil to the pan and fry the garlic and onions until soft. Add the beef stock, meat pieces, salt and pepper and combine.
- Lower the heat, cover and cook over gentle heat for approximately 1 hour and 30 minutes. Make sure to give the mix a stir every now and then to prevent it sticking at the bottom. The aim is to get the meat as tender as possible, so you may need to add a longer cooking time depending on the meat you buy.
- 10 minutes before the stew is cooked, add the finely sliced mushrooms and stir through to combine. Remove from the heat and allow to cool.
- Preheat the oven to 220°C/425°F/Gas Mark 7.
- Dust your work surface with a little flour and roll out the pastry to about ½ centimetre in thickness. Empty the steak and mushroom filling into your chosen pie dish or dishes and drape the pastry over it. Leave about 1cm of pastry over the side of the dish and then push the pastry down over the steak mix so you end up with a nice crust the whole way round. Using a pastry brush, brush the pastry with the egg yolk – this will produce a delicious, golden-coloured crust.
- Place in the oven for approximately 15–20 minutes or until the pastry puffs up and turns a nice golden brown.
- Serve straightaway with a tasty salad and enjoy! You could also cook the pie mix ahead of time, freeze and defrost when you want to use it.

Lamb Shanks

This is weekend cooking at its best. There is nothing like coming home to a house filled with the smell of lamb cooking in the oven. Lamb shanks can be ordered from your butcher if not readily on display. The lamb shanks are cooked until wonderfully tender and the meat practically falls off the bone.

Serves 4

4 lamb shanks
2 large carrots, chopped roughly
2 sticks of celery, chopped roughly
2 red onions, chopped roughly
4 garlic cloves, peeled and chopped roughly
200ml/7fl oz red wine
800ml/1½ pints water
1 tablespoon of sunflower oil
A small bunch of thyme, tied together with twine
A good pinch of sea salt and ground black pepper

- Preheat the oven to 180°C/350°F/Gas Mark 4.
- Heat a large casserole over a medium heat, add the sunflower oil, and fry the lamb shanks on all sides to seal. Try and get a colour on all sides of the shanks, then set aside on a plate.
- You may need to add an extra bit of oil to fry the vegetables, if so another tablespoon should do the job. Add the carrots, celery and onions, and fry for 2–3 minutes.
- Add the garlic, stir through and fry for a further minute. Return the lamb shanks to the pan and pour over the water and red wine.
- Place the bunch of thyme in the pan and season the lamb with salt and black pepper.
- Put the lid on the casserole and place in the oven. Cook for approximately 2 hours or until tender. Turn the lamb half way through the cooking time.
- Serve with my roast sweet potato and parsnip mash.

Thai Green Chicken Curry

This is a great dinner dish, perfect for when you have guests around. You can serve straight from the pot. Thai green curry paste and coconut milk are available in most good supermarkets. If you can't come across them, try an Asian food store.

Serves 4

4 chicken breasts, cut into thick strips
200g/7oz brown basmati rice
1 x 400g tin coconut milk
1 large onion, finely sliced
2 red peppers, sliced in strips
2 tablespoons of Thai green curry paste
1 tablespoon of sunflower oil
1 teaspoon of brown sugar
2 teaspoons of Thai fish sauce (Nam Pla)
Juice and zest of 1 lime
A handful of coriander, roughly chopped to serve

- Cook the rice according to the instructions on the packet while you prepare the green curry.
- In a medium frying pan, heat the oil and fry the onion and peppers for 2–3 minutes or until soft. Then add the green curry paste and cook for a further 1–2 minutes.
- Add the chicken and continue frying for 2 minutes.
- Add the coconut milk, brown sugar, Thai fish sauce, lime zest and bring to the boil.
- Lower the heat and simmer for 15–20 minutes or until the chicken is cooked and the sauce has reduced a little.
- Stir through the lime juice and serve with the brown basmati rice and a good sprinkle of coriander.

Bulgar Wheat, Chicken, Rocket and Parsley Salad

Originally a Middle Eastern ingredient, bulgar wheat is made from cracked wheat kernels. It's an excellent store cupboard ingredient which is highly nutritious and can be stored for long periods of time. This wholegrain product is packed with fibre and protein, but is low in calories, plus it's easy to make. This sort of recipe is perfect for entertaining; it can easily be made the night before and stored in the fridge.

Serves 4–6 people

200g/7oz bulgar wheat

3 chicken breasts

1 x 400g tin chickpeas, drained and roughly chopped

1 teaspoon of vegetable bouillon powder

3 tablespoons of extra virgin olive oil

1 tablespoon of balsamic vinegar

1 tablespoon of olive oil

A large handful of parsley, roughly chopped

A large handful of rocket, roughly chopped

A good pinch of sea salt and ground black pepper

- Place the bulgar wheat in a large bowl and cover with boiling water. Stir through the vegetable bouillon powder, cover with cloth or a cling film and allow to sit for about 30 minutes or until all the water is soaked up.
- Brush the chicken breasts with 1 tablespoon of olive oil and season with salt and black pepper.
- Heat a griddle pan over a high heat and just before it begins smoking add the chicken breasts. Reduce the heat slightly and cook on both sides for approximately 6–7 minutes depending on the size of the chicken breasts.
- Remove the chicken from the pan and roughly chop into bite-sized pieces.
- Add the chicken, parsley, rocket and chickpeas to the bulgar wheat, and stir through to combine.
- Season with an extra pinch of sea salt and ground black pepper and stir through the remaining olive oil and balsamic vinegar. Transfer to a serving dish and enjoy!

Real Baked Beans with Ciabatta

This is a pure indulgence and total comfort food for me. It's basically an upmarket version of beans on toast. It's the perfect sort of weekend food that can be produced from simple store-cupboard ingredients. If you don't want to go for the full bake on this, the beans and tomato sauce work well on thick slices of toast rubbed with a little garlic.

Serves 4

1 loaf of ciabatta bread
300g/11oz chorizo sausage, chopped
    into chunks
1 onion, roughly chopped
2 x 400g tins chopped tomatoes
125ml/4½fl oz red wine
2 x 400g tins cannellini beans, drained

2 balls of fresh mozzarella cheese
2 garlic cloves, finely chopped
1 tablespoon of olive oil
A good pinch of salt and pepper
A handful of fresh basil, roughly
    chopped

- Tear the ciabatta into large chunks, place in an ovenproof dish and set aside.
- In a medium-sized frying pan, fry the chorizo chunks until golden and set aside, retaining the rich oil.
- The chorizo slices will normally throw off enough oil in which to fry the onions, but if not just add a small drop of olive oil. Fry off the garlic and the onion for 2–3 minutes or until soft. Add the tomatoes and the red wine and bring to the boil. Lower the heat and simmer for 15–20 minutes or until the sauce has reduced.
- When the sauce has finished cooking, stir through the cannellini beans and the cooked chorizo chunks.
- Spoon the beans, chorizo and sauce mixture over the ciabatta, and combine so all the chunks are coated evenly. Roughly tear the mozzarella balls over the top of the dish and season with salt and pepper. Try to leave little peaks of the bread sticking out as this will allow parts of the dish to become nice and crispy.
- Bake in the oven for approximately 15–20 minutes at 200°C/400°F/Gas Mark 6, or until the cheese has turned golden brown.

Lime and Mint Mojito Chicken

One of my favourite cocktails is a mojito and, you guessed it, this recipe was thought up after one too many! But it was an experiment that paid off.

Serves 4 people

4 chicken breasts
1 garlic clove
4–5 tablespoons of white rum
Juice of 2 limes
2 limes quartered
1 tablespoon of olive oil
A small handful of fresh mint
A generous pinch of sea salt and freshly ground pepper

- Chop the mint and garlic finely and place in a large resealable bag. Add the rum, lime juice, oil, salt and pepper to the bag. I butterfly the chicken breasts so they cook quicker and the garlic doesn't burn. To do this, place one hand on the breast and with the other slice through the thickest part, making sure the breast stays attached on one side.
- Put the chicken in the bag and seal. Toss the chicken around in the bag and make sure the breasts are covered in the mint and garlic mixture.
- Leave in the fridge preferably overnight, or you can make it in the morning and leave for the day.
- To cook the chicken, heat a pan over a high heat and fry the breasts and marinade for about 3–5 minutes on either side, depending on the size of the chicken breasts.
- Tumble in the lime quarters after you turn the chicken and allow to caramelise on all sides. Serve straightaway with a tasty side salad, couscous and a final squeeze of juice from the caramelised lime quarters.

Sushi Made Simple:
Tuna Nigiri

I am a huge sushi fan, but it can be a bit too finicky to make at home. This is my solution. There are three main sushi types, with hundreds of variations. But for me, nigiri is basically the most stripped-down version of sushi you can get. If you can boil rice and use a knife you can make this. Try and buy the best quality tuna you can get — ideally ask your local fishmongers for sushi-grade tuna, but if they don't have it regular fresh tuna will do. I have kept this as simple as possible, but you can wrap thin strips of Nori (Japanese seaweed) around these little bundles if you want to give them that extra Japanese saltiness.

Serves 4

400g/14oz sushi rice
300g/10oz tuna steaks, sushi-grade if possible
100g/4oz sesame seeds
2 tablespoons of black peppercorns
1 teaspoon of sea salt
A drop of sunflower oil
Wasabi paste
Rice wine vinegar to season

To Serve:

Pickled ginger (also known as Gari), can be purchased in Asian supermarkets
Dipping bowl with soy sauce and finely chopped garlic

- Cook the sushi rice according to the instructions on the packet and cool on a large tray, season with a little rice wine vinegar and fork through.
- Mould into pieces, approximately 5cm long pieces, 2cm wide, 2cm high and set aside. You should make approximately 20 nigiri pieces.
- Keep a bowl of water beside you to dip your hands in before you make each little ball. The rice is very sticky so the water will allow you to work with it.

- In a pestle and mortar grind the sesame seeds, black peppercorns and sea salt. Lay the mix in a thin layer on a plate or chopping board and press down the tuna steaks so they are nicely coated on all sides.
- Heat a drop of sunflower oil in a large frying pan over a high heat. When the pan is smoking hot, fry the tuna steaks for 1 minute on both sides. Remove the steaks from the pan and allow to rest and cool.
- Slice into thin ½ cm pieces. The tuna should be roaring red in the middle and slightly pink at the edges.
- Spread each slice with a tiny smear of wasabi paste (be careful this stuff is HOT!), and place on top of the rice pieces.
- Serve the nigiri with pickled ginger and small bowl of dipping sauce made up of soy sauce and finely chopped garlic.

Caramelised Roast Vegetables

These herby root veggies, roasted tomatoes and caramelised onions make a perfect side dish to any main meal. You can even throw spaghetti into the cooked vegetables and serve as a yummy roast vegetable pasta dish.

Serves 4

2 large carrots, chopped into chunks
2 red onions, chopped roughly in quarters
8 baby potatoes, chopped in half
1 punnet of cherry tomatoes, chopped in half
2 tablespoons of olive oil
1 tablespoon of balsamic vinegar
1 tablespoon of honey
2 large sprigs of fresh rosemary
1 tablespoon of dried oregano
A good pinch of salt and pepper

- As an impressive side dish, this spends most of its cooking time in the oven so it's better to get the preparation for this out of the way before you begin anything else.
- Tumble all the vegetables into a large roasting tray and add the olive oil, balsamic vinegar and honey.
- Pinch the rosemary leaves off the stem and sprinkle over the vegetables, add the oregano, salt and pepper.
- Using your hands mix the herbs through the vegetables so they all have a nice herby coating.
- Cook in the oven at 200°C/400°F/Gas Mark 6, for approximately 45–50 minutes.
- Make sure to give the vegetables a good mix halfway through the cooking process so everything cooks evenly.

Mixed Vegetable Parmigiano

If, like me, you're a big fan of Italian lasagne, this is a perfect little healthy alternative which is just as tasty. Feel free to experiment by adding other vegetables to see what works. If you don't manage to eat it all in one serving, it's just as nice reheated the next day, mixed through some fresh pasta, and hey presto you have another great dish!

Serves 4

1 large aubergine
2 courgettes
200g/7oz goat's cheese
100g/3½oz parmesan cheese
2 tablespoons of olive oil
A good pinch of sea salt and ground
    black pepper
A handful of freshly chopped basil

For the tomato sauce:
2 x 400g tins chopped tomatoes
125ml/4½fl oz red wine
2 garlic cloves
1 red onion
2 teaspoons of dried oregano
A good splash of olive oil

- Slice the aubergine and courgette into thin slices about a ½ centimetre thick.
- Brush a coating of olive oil on both sides and grill for a couple of minutes either side until lightly brown. Set aside while you get on with the tomato sauce.
- In a large hot frying pan, fry the garlic and onion with a little oil until soft. Add the chopped tomatoes, oregano and red wine, and cook at a steady simmer for about 15 minutes, or until the sauce reduces.
- In a medium-sized roasting tin, spread a little tomato sauce over the bottom of the tin. Add a layer of the courgette and aubergine slices, and spread another layer of tomato sauce on top.
- Place slices of the goat's cheese and sprinkle the parmesan, salt, pepper and chopped basil on top. Continue to repeat the layers until you end up with the cheese and basil on top.
- Bake in an oven at 220°C/425°F/Gas Mark 7 for 20 minutes.

Mushy Roast Garlic and Cherry Tomato Pasta

Serves 4 people

250g/9oz wholewheat penne
1 large bulb of garlic
1 punnet of cherry tomatoes
1 large red onion
1 tablespoon of balsamic vinegar
3 tablespoons of olive oil
A good pinch of sea salt and ground black pepper
A large handful of grated parmesan cheese
An extra glug of olive oil

- Preheat the oven to 200°C/400°F/Gas Mark 6.
- Slice the top off the bulb of garlic so that almost all the cloves are exposed. Place the garlic in a large roasting tray.
- Prepare the cherry tomatoes by slicing them in half. Place the tomatoes in the roasting tray. Prepare the red onion by peeling and slicing into rough quarters, place alongside the tomatoes and set aside.
- In a separate bowl, mix together the balsamic vinegar and olive oil and using a pastry brush, brush the mix over the tomatoes, the red onion and garlic bulb. Sprinkle the tomatoes, garlic and onion with a good pinch of sea salt and black pepper. Roast in the oven for 30–35 minutes or until the tomatoes have reduced to half their size.
- While the garlic, tomatoes and onion are roasting, bring a medium-sized pot of water to the boil and cook the pasta according to the instructions on the packet. Drain the pasta in a colander and set aside.
- When the tomatoes, garlic and onion are cooked, remove from the oven and, using a fork, carefully push out the garlic cloves from their skins and mash all the ingredients together until you have a thick mushy sauce. Tumble the cooked pasta into the roasting tray and add the parmesan cheese and an extra glug of olive oil. Toss everything together until the pasta is evenly coated. Serve in a large bowl and enjoy!

Asian Rice Rolls

I make a big batch of these to snack on with a little soy dipping sauce. Now I will admit that unless you have been making these delicious rice noodle rolls under the instruction of an old Chinese mama from a young age, it's a little tricky. However, once you get the hang of these, you will never look back, and what guest wouldn't be impressed with home made rice rolls! You can pick up the rice roll discs at any decent Asian supermarket and they are fairly cheap too. If I don't have the discs to hand, I sometimes make this as a tasty noodle dish.

Serves 4

100g/4oz rice vermicelli noodles
100g/4oz bean sprouts
125g/4½oz cooked prawns
4 spring onions, finely sliced
½ cucumber, finely sliced
Packet of rice paper discs
A small handful of freshly chopped
  coriander

For the dressing:

1 tablespoon of sunflower oil
1 tablespoon of rice wine vinegar
2 tablespoons of soy sauce
1 tablespoon of fish sauce
½ teaspoon of sugar
1 garlic clove, finely chopped
½ red chilli, finely chopped
Juice of ½ lime

- Soak the rice vermicelli noodles according to instructions on the packet then drain and set aside.
- In a small container with a lid, place all the ingredients for the dressing. Cover the container and give it a good shake, then set aside.
- Now you can get on with the filling for the rice rolls. Place the cucumber, spring onions, bean sprouts, rice vermicelli, prawns and coriander in a large bowl. Add in the dressing and toss to combine.
- In a large bowl of warm water soften the rice discs according to the instructions on the packet. Pat each one dry on a clean tea towel.
- Place a heaped tablespoon of the filling onto the centre of the rice papers. Spread in a thin line, tuck in at the sides and roll up like a tortilla wrap.
- Serve these little rolls on a large serving platter with extra soy sauce in small bowls for dipping.

Real Fast Food

Real Fast Food

There is plenty of coverage in the media these days about fast food and its negative effect on health and wellbeing, as well as its contribution to rising obesity levels. It's packed full of sugar, salt and artificial additives and other undesirable ingredients. But fast food doesn't have to mean junk food. The real fast food is food which is easy to prepare, digests easily and won't leave you feeling sluggish. When I am in need of a quick and tasty fix these are just some of my favourite recipes which are easy to throw together any time and always leave me more than satisfied. Better than a frozen pizza or take away any day!

These dishes really come into their own when you have a well stocked store cupboard, so you don't have to go too far to make a delicious meal (see page 22 for 'Store Cupboard Essentials' suggestions). My other solution to fast food is freezing ahead – soups and marinated meats can be frozen and quickly defrosted when you need them (see page 25 for 'My Freezer Essentials' suggestions).

Lots of the recipes in this chapter can easily be adapted to whatever vegetables you might have in your fridge, so if you don't have all the ingredients for a certain salad or a rice dish, experiment by adding and subtracting to suit your own taste.

Building a repertoire of recipes that you can easily turn to when you are hungry is the key to eating healthily, and means you are more likely to avoid eating processed fast foods with little nutritional value.

Spiced Sweet Potato and Squash Soup

The combination of sweet potato and squash results in a really rich, velvet-textured soup and a fantastic golden colour. This is a soup to which you can add other vegetables quite easily. Carrot, celery, potato and parsnip all work really well in this recipe, so if you have them in the kitchen, don't be afraid to make additions! This soup also freezes really well.

Serves 4

1 small butternut squash, peeled and chopped into chunks
3 sweet potatoes, peeled and chopped into chunks
1 litre/2 pints vegetable stock
2 garlic cloves, finely chopped
1 thumb-sized piece of ginger, peeled and roughly chopped
2 teaspoons of dried thyme
1 medium onion, coarsely chopped
1 tablespoon of olive oil
A good pinch of sea salt and ground black pepper

- In a large pot, heat the olive oil and add the onion. Fry for 2 minutes until the onion has softened. Then add the garlic, ginger, black pepper and thyme, and fry for a further 30–40 seconds.
- At this point add the squash and sweet potato, and cook for a further 3 minutes. Add the stock and bring to the boil, reduce the heat and simmer for 20–25 minutes, or until the vegetables are soft when pressed with a fork.
- Remove from the heat and using a hand blender, blitz to a silky, velvet texture.
- Season with salt and pepper and serve straightaway with wholegrain bread, or divide into individual plastic resealable bags and stick in the freezer.

Spicy Herb Pasta

Most pasta dishes I cook tend to be made in a hurry, with hungry bellies waiting! This is a perfect example of a tasty pasta dish which can be thrown together in minutes and is packed with flavour. I use basil as my main herb here, but you can also add coarsely chopped parsley, to give it extra herbiness. The pangrattato is basically fancy Italian breadcrumbs, for want of a more elaborate explanation. It adds the perfect crunch and texture to this dish, which is a nice complement to the garlicy pasta.

Serves 4

450g/1lb wholewheat spaghetti
2 garlic cloves, peeled
A large handful of basil
A large handful of parsley
1 tablespoon of olive oil
Juice of 1 lemon

For the Pangrattato:

2–3 chunky pieces of stale wholemeal
    bread
1 garlic clove
1 red chilli, deseeded and finely chopped
1 sprig of fresh rosemary
A good glug of olive oil

- For the pangrattato, give the bread and garlic a quick whizz in a food processor so you have breadcrumbs with a bit of texture.
- In a large frying pan heat a generous glug of olive oil until hot. Add the whole rosemary sprig and the chilli, and fry for about 1–2 minutes.
- Add the breadcrumbs and continue to cook for a couple of minutes until they become crisp and golden. Set aside on a plate on a sheet of kitchen paper, which will soak up any excess oil and leave the savoury crumbs nice and crispy. Discard the rosemary sprig.
- Bring a large pot of water to the boil, add the spaghetti and cook according to the instructions on the packet.
- While the spaghetti is cooking, mince the garlic, and chop the basil and parsley roughly on a chopping board.
- Drain the pasta and drizzle with olive oil, adding the freshly chopped herbs and garlic and give a good stir so they are thoroughly mixed.
- Serve in a large pasta bowl topped with the pangrattato and a good squeeze of lemon.

Turkey and Kidney Bean Chilli

This chilli can be frozen and reheated quite successfully for a quick no fuss dinner. Turkey mince is a healthy replacement for minced beef in this dish and can be bought quite easily at most good supermarkets or butchers.

Serves 4

500g/1lb turkey mince
2 x 400g tins chopped tomatoes
1 x 400g tin kidney beans
2 garlic cloves, finely chopped
2 medium onions, finely chopped
2 red peppers, finely chopped
2 tablespoons of chilli powder
2 teaspoons of ground cumin
1 teaspoon of dried oregano
1 tablespoon of sunflower oil
Sour cream, wholemeal wraps and chopped parsley to serve

- In a large pot, heat the oil and fry the garlic, red pepper and onions for 3–4 minutes. Add the turkey mince and fry for a further 4 minutes until the turkey is no longer pink.
- Stir through the chilli powder, cumin and oregano, and then add the tomatoes. Bring the chilli to the boil, reduce the heat and simmer for at least 30 minutes, stirring every now and then. The longer you cook the chilli the deeper the flavour.
- Add the beans, stir through and cook for a further 5 minutes or until they are heated through.
- Divide the chilli into bowls and serve with a dollop of low fat sour cream and a sprinkle of parsley.
- This chilli is also ideal to use with wholemeal tortilla wraps as a tasty lunch.

Sunblush Tomato, Basil and Goat's Cheese Pasta

A wonderful dish which can be made in a matter of minutes. This punchy combination of flavours makes for a perfect quick dinner. Sunblush tomatoes are quite easy to pick up and can be found stored in jars or you can ask for them at deli counters in most good supermarkets.

Serves 4

250g/9oz wholewheat penne pasta
150g/5oz sunblush tomatoes (plus a little of the oil they are stored in)
75g/3oz goat's cheese
A handful of fresh basil leaves
A good pinch of sea salt
A few slices of good crunchy toasted bread to serve

- Bring a large pot of water to the boil and cook the pasta according to instructions on the packet.
- While the pasta is cooking, remove the tomatoes from the oil they are stored in and set the oil aside to add to the pasta later.
- Roughly chop the basil leaves and sunblush tomatoes and set aside.
- When the pasta is cooked, drain in a colander and put back in the pot.
- Drizzle with the tomato oil and add the basil and sunblush tomatoes, stir to combine.
- Crumble in the goat's cheese, season with a little sea salt and, using a large serving spoon, stir the cheese through the pasta.
- Serve straightaway or this also works really well as a tasty lunch box filler.

Prawn and Potato Basil Salad

This is a really tasty and fragrant salad, which you can serve with any salad leaves really. However, I use rocket and watercress which both have a deeper taste and peppery kick than regular salad leaves. I sometimes add a few roughly chopped hard-boiled eggs to this recipe.

Serves 2

12 baby potatoes
200g/7oz cooked and peeled prawns
A large handful of fresh watercress
A large handful of fresh rocket
A good handful of fresh dill, roughly chopped
A good handful of fresh basil, roughly chopped
2 heaped tablespoons of Greek yoghurt
2 tablespoons of extra virgin olive oil
1 teaspoon of English mustard powder
Juice and zest of 1 lemon
Sea salt and freshly ground pepper

- In a large pot cover the potatoes with boiling water, cover with a lid and bring to the boil. Cook the potatoes for approximately 10–15 minutes or until tender – you can test them with a fork. Drain and set aside.
- While the potatoes are cooking, prepare the rest of the salad. In a large mixing bowl, combine the Greek yoghurt with the olive oil, mustard, dill, basil, lemon zest, juice and prawns.
- Chop the cooked baby potatoes into chunks and don't be too concerned if they break up during the process.
- Place them into the bowl with the Greek yoghurt dressing and mix through so that all the potatoes have a nice coating.
- Serve on a large platter on top of a bed of watercress and rocket leaves. Top with a good sprinkle of sea salt and freshly ground pepper.

Roast Potato and Carrot Salad

There is something about any food cooked in a roasting tin that can quickly conjure up feelings of comfort and home, and roast potatoes and carrots in particular create for me that warm feeling. I actually came up with this dish during the summer because I had a hankering for some roast vegetables, but felt they might be a little out of place on a warm July evening.

Serves 2

2 large carrots
10 baby potatoes
2 tablespoons of honey
1 tablespoon of olive oil
1 teaspoon of dried chilli flakes
A handful of fresh rosemary
A few sprigs of thyme
A good selection of mixed salad leaves

A good pinch of salt and pepper

For the dressing:
1 small garlic clove
One handful of parsley
3 tablespoons of olive oil
1 tablespoon of balsamic vinegar
A good pinch of salt and pepper

- Preheat the oven to 220°C/425°F/Gas Mark 7.
- Peel and chop the carrots and potatoes (skin on) into hefty chunks, and throw into a large roasting tray. Drizzle the honey and olive oil over the chunks and then dust with the chilli flakes, salt, pepper, chopped rosemary and thyme. Cook in the oven for approximately 40 minutes, turning the mix about three times throughout.
- While the vegetables are roasting, prepare the salad leaves in a large bowl. The dressing is very simple, but complements the sweetness of the carrots and adds an extra bite to the potato.
- Smash the garlic and chop finely with the parsley, add the mix to something you can shake the dressing in (I find a jam jar with a lid does the trick) and combine with the olive oil and balsamic vinegar. Add a little pinch of salt and pepper to taste and give it good shake.
- When the vegetables are cooked, tumble them into the salad bowl and drizzle over the dressing. The heat from the vegetables will wilt the salad leaves so if you're going to combine them, make sure to serve straightaway.

Roast Squash Spaghetti

This has to be one of my favourite quick fix meals. It's packed with flavour and butternut squash is one of my favourite superfoods. There is something extremely satisfying about tumbling tender cooked pasta into a roasting tray and soaking up all the intense flavours — I love how the squash almost becomes a spicy mush and coats the pasta perfectly!

Serves 2

200g/7oz wholewheat spaghetti
1 butternut squash
1 punnet of cherry tomatoes
A handful of pancetta, chopped into bite-size chunks, or bacon bits
1 tablespoon of olive oil
1 tablespoon of honey
1 teaspoon of dried chilli flakes
1 teaspoon of cinnamon
A handful of freshly chopped basil
A good pinch of sea salt and freshly ground pepper

- If you've never come across a butternut squash before, it can be tricky vegetable to get to grips with. In order to peel it, the best thing to do (and the safest) is to separate the top from the bottom.
- Remove the seeds with a spoon and using a sharp knife cut away the thick skin from top to bottom. Slice into length-way pieces and put in a large roasting tin.
- Add the cherry tomatoes and pancetta pieces on top and coat with the olive oil, honey, salt, pepper, dried chilli flakes and cinnamon. Roast in an oven for approximately 30 minutes at 220°C/425°F/Gas Mark 7.
- Fifteen minutes before the squash is finished roasting, cook the spaghetti and keep warm. When the squash is ready, put the spaghetti on top in the roasting tray and throw in some freshly chopped basil. The squash should be soft at this stage, so don't be afraid to break it up while mixing with the spaghetti. This looks good enough to serve straight from the roasting tray at the table.

Spicy Sweet Potato Chips

These sweet and spicy little wedges knock the socks off greasy fast food chips any day. If you haven't tried sweet potatoes before, this is a great introduction recipe, where you just can't go wrong. Serve as a nice side dish or a quick and tasty snack!

Serves 4

5 large sweet potatoes
2 garlic cloves, finely chopped
3 tablespoons of sunflower oil
1 teaspoon of dried oregano
1 teaspoon of ground cumin
½ teaspoon of dried red chilli flakes
1 teaspoon of sea salt
1 teaspoon of freshly ground black pepper

- Preheat the oven to 190°C/375°F/Gas Mark 5.
- If I am serving these as a side dish, I generally prepare them first and let them cook away in the oven while I get on with the rest of the dinner.
- Peel the sweet potatoes and slice in half lengthways and then in half again, then chop into rough chips.
- Place in a large roasting tin and toss the wedges with oil and the remaining ingredients until all the chips are well coated.
- Roast in the oven for about 40–45 minutes, or until the insides are soft and the edges are slightly charred.

Homemade Paprika Roast Potato Chips

When it comes to snack foods, everyone has their weakness — mine just happens to be these homemade potato chips.

Makes enough for 4 portions, or one giant selfish one!

5 rooster potatoes
3 tablespoons of olive oil
2 teaspoons of paprika
1 tablespoon of ground black pepper
1 tablespoon of sea salt

- Preheat the oven to 200°C/400°F/Gas Mark 6.
- Leaving the skins on, cut the potatoes into chips about 1cm in thickness.
- Spread the potato chips evenly over two large non-stick baking trays. Try and give the chips as much space as possible, this will make them extra crispy.
- Drizzle the oil over the chips and toss until they are all covered. Sprinkle over the paprika, pepper, salt and toss again.
- Place in the oven and roast for 40–50 minutes or until crispy and golden.
- Serve straightaway as a tasty snack or alongside a main meal.

Healthy Egg Fried Rice

When I come home from work, this is a classic 'throw together meal'. The recipe here is my standard version, but more often than not, ingredients are added and subtracted depending on what's in the kitchen. It's also a great way to use up leftover vegetables in the fridge. I always make a little extra, to stick in a lunch box for the next day.

Serves 4

200g/7oz brown basmati rice
2 eggs
1 red pepper, finely chopped
2 bunches of spring onions, thinly sliced
2 large carrots, thinly sliced
2 large handfuls of bean sprouts
1 tablespoon of sunflower oil
1 teaspoon of sesame oil

2 garlic cloves, peeled and finely grated
1 red chilli, deseeded and finely chopped
1 thumb-sized piece of ginger, peeled and finely grated
1 tablespoon of soy sauce
1 tablespoon of fish sauce

- Follow the instructions on the packet to cook the rice and set aside.
- While the rice is cooking, prepare the rest of the ingredients. Lightly whisk the 2 eggs in a bowl and set aside.
- In a large frying pan, heat the sunflower oil, add the garlic, chilli, ginger, and stir-fry for 1 minute.
- Add the red pepper, spring onions, carrots and bean sprouts, and stir-fry for a further 3 minutes.
- Add the sesame oil, soy sauce and Thai fish sauce (Nam Pla), and stir through the vegetables for 1 more minute.
- Add the rice to the pan and combine with the vegetables.
- Make a well and pour in the whisked egg. Allow to set briefly, then working quickly, stir the egg and quickly incorporate the rice from the sides until everything is combined.
- Cook for 2 minutes and serve straightaway in a big bowl for quick and tasty dinner!

Garlic, Mushroom and Goat's Cheese Pasta

Garlic and mushroom is a classic combination and works perfectly in this tasty pasta dish. Crumbling the goat's cheese over the hot pasta creates a creamy coating and leaves the dish with a distinctive tangy taste.

Serves 4 people

250g/9oz wholewheat penne
150g/5oz mushrooms sliced thinly (approximately 6 large mushrooms)
75g/3oz goat's cheese
1 tablespoon of olive oil
3 garlic cloves, finely chopped
1 onion, chopped into thin half-moon slices
A generous pinch of black pepper
A generous pinch of sea salt

- Bring a large pot of water to the boil and add the pasta and cook according to the instructions on the pack. While the pasta is cooking prepare the garlic and onion.
- In a large frying pan heat the oil, add the garlic and onion, and fry gently until softened and browned.
- Then add the mushrooms and cook until soft.
- When the pasta is cooked drain in a colander and put back in the pot.
- Drizzle with a little extra olive oil and add the mushrooms, garlic and onion.
- Crumble in the goat's cheese, add the salt and pepper, and stir together until everything is combined evenly.
- Serve straightaway in deep dishes and season with a little extra black pepper.

Balsamic Chicken with Avocado and Radish Salad

Serves 2

2 free range chicken breasts

1 tablespoon of balsamic vinegar

3 tablespoons of olive oil

Juice of ½ lemon

A good pinch of black pepper

1 red onion, cut in half and sliced wafer thin

1 avocado

6 radishes

A large handful of oak leaf lettuce leaves

For the dressing:

1 tablespoons of balsamic vinegar

3 tablespoons of extra virgin olive oil

1 small garlic clove, finely chopped

1 teaspoon of wholegrain mustard

Juice of ½ lemon

A good pinch of sea salt

- If you have the time to marinate the chicken breasts overnight, by all means go ahead. Remove any fat or skin from the breasts and place in small resealable bag. Pour in 1 tablespoon of balsamic vinegar, 3 tablespoons of olive oil, the juice of half a lemon and a pinch of black pepper. Seal and give a good shake.
- In a jar, bowl, or whatever you want to make your dressing in, combine the dressing ingredients. Whisk or shake to combine and set aside.
- Heat a large frying pan, until just before it begins smoking, and place the chicken on it. You shouldn't need any extra oil as olive oil is used in the marinade. Cook for approximately 4–5 minutes either side then remove from the heat. Let it rest for a few minutes (if you can wait) and slice into thin strips.
- Place a good handful of lettuce leaves on each plate and scatter with the red onion.
- Slice the avocado in half and remove the stone. Spoon out the green flesh, slice into thin strips and arrange on top of the salad. Give them a squeeze of lemon juice to prevent browning. Cut the radishes into quarters and place on the outside of the plate.
- Arrange the chicken strips on top of the avocado and using a spoon drizzle the dressing over the salad.

Dry Rub Lamb Chops with Watercress Salad

Try to get really good lamb chops for this recipe, nice pink ones with creamy white fat; you should have a good selection at your local butcher.

Serves 2

4 lamb chops
3 teaspoons of dried oregano
1 teaspoon of chilli powder
1 teaspoon of ground cumin
1 teaspoon of ground cinnamon
2 garlic cloves, finely chopped
A handful of watercress per person
A good pinch of sea salt and black
  pepper

For the dressing:
1 garlic clove, finely chopped
1 teaspoon of Dijon mustard
3 tablespoon of extra virgin olive oil
1 tablespoon of cider vinegar

- Combine the oregano, chilli powder, cumin, cinnamon, garlic, salt and black pepper on a large plate.
- Press all sides of the lamb chops onto the mixture, which will stick nicely to the meat.
- Place the chops under a hot grill and cook for 4–5 minutes either side, or until the meat gets a good colour.
- Combine the dressing ingredients and mix. Toss the watercress in the dressing.
- Serve the lamb chops with the watercress salad on the side and dig in!

Broccoli, Feta and Cherry Tomato Salad

I love chunky salads like this; I often make a big batch and then pick at it from the fridge. For vegetarians, it is just as tasty without the pancetta or bacon.

Serves 4 people

1 large head of broccoli, chopped into bite-size pieces
1 punnet of cherry tomatoes
1 x 125g packet of ready chopped pancetta or bacon
100g crumbled feta cheese
3 tablespoons of extra virgin olive oil
1 tablespoon of balsamic vinegar
A good pinch of sea salt and of ground black pepper

- Bring a large pot of water to the boil. While the water is boiling, combine the olive oil and balsamic vinegar in a serving bowl.
- Add the broccoli to the pot of water and blanch for 60 seconds – you should see the broccoli turn a vibrant green.
- Drain the broccoli pieces and run under cold water. Add the broccoli to the serving bowl and set aside.
- Place a small frying pan over a high heat and fry the bacon/pancetta pieces until crispy. Remove the bacon from the pan, place on some kitchen paper and allow to cool before adding to the rest of salad.
- Slice the cherry tomatoes in half and tumble into the bowl on top of the broccoli.
- Add the bacon pieces and feta cheese to the serving bowl.
- Gently toss with the olive oil and balsamic vinegar and season with sea salt and black pepper. Serve as a tasty side dish or a really tasty lunch.
- You can also add walnuts or pine nuts for extra crunch!

Healing and
Recovery Food

Healing and Recovery Food

Food is one of the oldest natural healing tools; it has so many uses and the ability to repair, boost and heal. Even on the worst of days, a big bowl of soup or a fresh juice can totally change our outlook and make things feel that little bit better.

Even the common cold can be tackled with a little bit of care and the right food.

Most common everyday illnesses, like colds and infections, can be avoided by strengthening the immune system over a period of time. Eating the right foods and making sure to include fresh fruit and vegetables in your diet can really help, but sometimes, depending on your lifestyle, your body can just become run down.

One of the best pieces of advice I was ever given, was to always listen to your body – it will almost always let you know when something is wrong. Now, at the first sign of a tickle in my throat, or a headache, I fill myself with foods packed with nutrients to give my body every chance of fighting infection.

The recipes in this chapter are some of my favourite little vitamin boosters, and some are just comfort food perfect for 'duvet days'! I often make double quantities of these recipes so that I can pick at them throughout the day, and many of the soups can be frozen ahead of time for use when required.

Chicken Noodle Soup

The ingredients used in this recipe are all super healthy and provide lots of antioxidants. Many studies have shown that the powerful nutrients of shitake mushrooms, ginger and garlic, which have all been used in traditional Chinese medicine for thousands of years, have positive effects on blood pressure, digestive problems, and lowers cholesterol. All that and they taste great too! If you have any leftover roast chicken, you can use that here, instead of poaching the chicken in this recipe.

Serves 4

2 chicken breasts
225g/8oz wholewheat noodles, cooked
2 pak choy, coarsely chopped
A handful of shitake mushrooms
800ml/1½ pints homemade chicken stock
1 star anise
1 garlic clove, finely chopped

1 thumb-sized piece of ginger, finely chopped
2 tablespoons of soy sauce
1 tablespoon of rice wine vinegar
1 handful of spring onions, sliced thinly on the diagonal
1 handful of finely chopped coriander leaves
Sesame oil to serve

- Bring the stock to the boil in a large pot and add the chicken and star anise. Poach the chicken for 15–20 minutes or until cooked through. Remove the breasts and set aside to cool.
- While the chicken is poaching, cook the noodles according to the instructions on the packet. Drain and rinse under cold water. Set aside.
- Bring the stock back to the boil and add the pak choy, shitake mushrooms, garlic, ginger, soy sauce and rice wine vinegar.
- Add the noodles and simmer while you prepare the chicken.
- Slice the chicken breasts thinly and add them to the soup to warm through.
- To serve, divide the noodles, chicken and vegetables evenly between the serving bowls and ladle over the broth. Top with some coriander, spring onions and a drizzle of sesame oil.

Pea and Mint Soup

Pea and mint has to be one of the best flavour combinations in the world. This is such a hearty warming soup full of antioxidants. Peas, particularly frozen, are one of the original superfoods and they're packed with vitamins and minerals. Mint has long been associated with aiding digestion and can prevent inflammation. This is one of my staple soups which I make up the night before I eat it. The next morning it is perfect to heat up and pour into a flask for a simple and almost effortless lunch.

Serves 4

500g/1lb frozen garden peas
2 garlic cloves, finely chopped
2 large onions, finely chopped
1 litre/2 pints vegetable stock
A large handful of fresh mint leaves
1 tablespoon of olive oil
A pinch of sea salt and black pepper

- In a large pot, fry the onions and garlic in the olive oil for about 2 minutes.
- Add the peas allowing them to soften for a further 2 minutes. Stir through the mint leaves and continue to cook for another minute.
- Add the vegetable stock and bring to the boil, reduce the heat and simmer uncovered for 15–20 minutes.
- Whizz the soup with a hand blender or in a food processor.
- Season with a little sea salt and black pepper.
- Serve the soup straightaway in a large bowl and with a sprig of mint. I often save extra portions in small freezer bags, which will last for about a month.

Red Pepper Soup

This has to be the ultimate winter warming soup – it's bursting with Vitamin C and all the antioxidants that tomatoes and red peppers have to offer. I use thyme and dried oregano, but experiment with whatever you have in the kitchen, and don't be afraid to add other vegetables. When it comes to soups I tend to make a big batch at the start of the week which will generally do me for the week. It will last the five days in the fridge or you can also freeze portions in little airtight bags, which can be defrosted and reheated when needed. The flavour won't be too affected during the freezing and thawing.

Serves 4

8 red peppers, chopped into chunks
4 large tomatoes, chopped roughly
1 litre/2 pints vegetable stock
2 tablespoons of olive oil
2 onions, chopped
2 garlic cloves, crushed
2 teaspoons of dried oregano
2 teaspoons of chopped fresh thyme
1 teaspoon of red chilli flakes
Sea salt and freshly ground pepper

- Heat the olive oil in a large pot. Add the onions and cook until they begin to soften. Then add garlic and continue to cook for a further minute.
- Add the peppers and tomatoes to the pot and stir through with the onions and garlic.
- Pour the stock into the pot and add the oregano, thyme, chilli flakes, salt and pepper.
- Bring the soup to the boil, then reduce the heat and simmer for about 25 minutes, until both peppers and tomatoes are tender.
- You can either serve as a chunky broth or puree for a silky warm soup.

Carrot, Ginger and Cumin Soup

Ginger, for me, gives any dish an almost instant health boost and I can't get enough of the stuff! The extra little pinch of curry powder also gives this soup a really great kick of flavour.

Serves 4

6 large carrots, chopped roughly
2 onions, roughly chopped
1 litre/2 pints vegetable stock
2 thumb-sized pieces of ginger, peeled and finely chopped
1 tablespoon of butter
2 teaspoons of ground cumin
1 teaspoon of curry powder
A good pinch of salt and pepper
A handful of freshly chopped parsley

- In a large pot, melt the butter and add the onions, sauté for approximately 2 minutes or until golden.
- While they are frying add in the ginger, cumin and curry powder. You will really see the colours of the spices come alive. Tumble in the carrots and stir amongst the onion over a medium heat for a further 4 minutes.
- Add the stock and bring to the boil. Put on a lid and simmer for 25–30 minutes or until the carrot chunks are tender. Season with a little sea salt and black pepper.
- You can serve the soup as it is for a chunky hearty soup or blitz to a puree and garnish with a handful of freshly chopped parsley.

Ultimate Vitamin C Booster!

The first thing I do the minute I feel a cold coming on, is make this fantastic drink packed with Vitamin C. I'm a true believer that most common illnesses can be warded off with a bit of careful eating and rest. Lemons have long been known as a natural disinfectant and a powerful source of vitamins, perfect for when your body is feeling run down.

Serves 2

½ pineapple chopped into chunks
Juice of 3 oranges
Juice of one lemon
1 tablespoon of honey

- This takes less than 5 minutes. In a blender or with a hand blender, blitz the pineapple chunks, the juice of 3 oranges, the juice of one lemon and a tablespoon of honey.
- Serve straightaway or chill in the fridge and continue to drink throughout the day.

Raw Food Salad

This has to be my ultimate health food salad. Don't be put off by all the raw ingredients — some people are a bit unsure about raw fennel, but it's actually quite subtle in this salad.

Serves 4

½ head of cabbage
1 head of broccoli
½ red onion
1 small fennel bulb
1 cucumber
1 large carrot
1 red pepper
1 teaspoon of Dijon mustard
3 tablespoons of extra virgin olive oil
1 tablespoon of balsamic vinegar
A good pinch of ground pepper and coarse sea salt

- Shred the cabbage finely and sprinkle into a large salad bowl.
- Remove the broccoli florets from the stalk, and dice finely, add to the bowl.
- If you have a vegetable slicer or a mandolin, now is an excellent time to use it; if not, slice the onion, fennel and cucumber into wafer thin slices, and add to the bowl.
- Finely dice the carrot and pepper, and add to the bowl.
- Combine the mustard, olive oil and balsamic vinegar in a small bowl, and pour over the vegetables.
- Season with sea salt and black pepper and give the salad a really good toss so that all the vegetables are coated thoroughly.
- Serve as a side salad or in a large bowl as a generous main salad.

Chicken and Sweetcorn Soup

My mom used to make this super tasty soup for us when we were kids. It has become a classic in our house, always being requested on sick days home from school. I always find sweetcorn lends a warm and comforting taste to soups and its bright colour puts a smile on my face. Try not to skimp on ingredients for this one, it tastes best when you use the best ingredients — homemade stock and fresh ginger are a must! If you have any leftover roast chicken, you can use that here, instead of poaching the chicken in this recipe.

Serves 4

2 large free range chicken breasts
1 litre/2 pints of homemade chicken
    stock
2 x 400g tins sweetcorn
1 tablespoon of sunflower oil
1 thumb-sized piece of ginger, finely
    chopped

2 garlic cloves, finely chopped
1 tablespoon of soy sauce
1 tablespoon of rice wine vinegar
1 teaspoon of sesame oil
2 eggs lightly beaten
4 spring onions finely sliced diagonally

- Split the chicken breasts horizontally and place in a pot with the chicken stock.
- Bring the stock to the boil, then remove from the heat and allow the chicken to continue to cook in the liquid as it cools for about 20 minutes. Remove the chicken and pat dry, shred with a fork and set aside.
- In a large pot with a little oil, fry the garlic and ginger for about 3 minutes, add the corn and cook for a further 3 minutes.
- Add a little bit of the chicken stock and, with a hand blender, blitz the mixture until it becomes smooth.
- Add the rest of the chicken stock, soy sauce, rice wine vinegar and sesame oil. Bring to the boil, and simmer for 10 minutes.
- While the soup is still simmering, stir it continuously in a figure of eight motion and gently trickle in the beaten egg a little bit at a time to form thin strands.
- Add the chicken shreds and stir through. Serve with a generous garnish of spring onions.

Hearty Minestrone

This is a perfect winter meal solution, full of tasty vegetables, and filling thanks to the pasta. I use wholewheat spaghetti, but feel free to add other shapes like fusilli or pasta elbows instead. If you don't have any paprika, you can get a bit of spice by adding a dash of Tabasco sauce, or a good pinch of dried chilli flakes.

Serves 4

1 courgette, chopped into small chunks
1 x 400g tin chopped tomatoes
2 x 410g tins cannellini beans
2 garlic cloves, finely chopped
1 large onion, finely chopped
2 stalks of celery, chopped
2 large carrots, chopped into small chunks
2 litres/4 pints homemade chicken stock
75g/3oz wholewheat spaghetti, broken into 1-inch pieces
2 tablespoons of olive oil
A good pinch of paprika
A good pinch of sea salt

- In a large pot, heat the olive oil and fry the garlic cloves and onion for 2 minutes or until they become soft.
- Stir in the celery, carrots and courgette and cook for five minutes. Add the chopped tomatoes and chicken stock, and bring to the boil, then reduce the heat and simmer for 20 minutes.
- Add the wholewheat spaghetti, paprika and cannellini beans. Give the soup a good stir and cover. Cook gently for a further 10 minutes or until the pasta is cooked.
- Season with a little sea salt and serve straightaway with a good chunk of wholemeal bread and enjoy!

Sweets and Treats

Sweets and Treats

Desserts are the best ending to the perfect meal. I love desserts which wow people and will always make sure they have room for more. There's nothing better than putting a smile on people's faces with your choice of dessert. Take cupcakes for example: I have never seen a better reaction from one item of food in all the time I have been cooking. When a plate of cupcakes enter a room, eyes light up, people make strange noises and adults are quickly reduced to children when they have to make their selection!

This collection of desserts is made with healthy and wholesome ingredients so you shouldn't feel too guilty in the making or the eating.

My answer to healthy desserts is fruit – pack as much of it into your desserts as you can and you won't have to feel guilty about finding space for a little extra! There are so many options to choose from and baking fruit can really bring out its natural sweetness.

Most popular desserts can be adapted to a healthy diet, and by including wholegrain or wholemeal ingredients you can easily increase the health benefits. So try adapting some of your favourite recipes and you'll surprise yourself with the results.

A lot of the dishes in this chapter are easy to put together, so even if you haven't planned for them you should be able to easily produce something really tasty at the end of dinner. I did try to keep the recipes in this chapter as healthy as possible, but a few sinful treats did creep in!

Grilled Pineapple skewers with Caramelised Mint Sugar

This is a super summer dessert, perfect for the barbecue! It works just as well under a hot grill for cold winter months too. When selecting pineapples, try to look for fruit with deep green leaves, a fresh sweet smell and the fruit should feel heavier than it looks.

Serves 4

1 pineapple cut in lengthway strips
6 tablespoons of Demerara sugar
14–16 mint leaves finely chopped

- Skewer all the pineapple strips and set aside.
- In a food processor or a pestle and mortar, blitz the Demerara sugar and mint leaves until they are combined.
- Spread the sugar mint mix out on a large plate. Place each of the pineapple skewers on the sugar and mint mixture, and coat all sides evenly.
- Place the skewers under a hot grill, and allow the sugar to caramelise. Turn until you have an even golden brown colour on all sides.
- Serve straightaway.

Cookies and Cream Chocolate Chip Oreo Cupcakes

I had to include this — I couldn't resist! My brother and I were a little bit obsessed with Oreo cookies when we were kids. They only arrived on Ireland's green shores in the late 1990s commercially, and they quickly became the coolest thing to have in your school lunch box at the time. This is my Auntie Erica's cupcake recipe and it could not be easier to make. You can easily adapt this recipe to make a regular plain cupcake mixture, simply remove the cocoa powder and chocolate chips from the ingredients.

Makes approximately 8 cupcakes

175g/6oz self raising flour
110g/4oz caster sugar
110g/4oz soft margarine or butter
50ml/2fl oz milk or water
50g/2oz good quality chocolate chips
2 tablespoons of cocoa powder
1 teaspoon of baking powder

2 large eggs

For the Oreo cream frosting:
250ml/8½fl oz fresh cream
25g/1oz icing sugar
½ teaspoon of vanilla extract
8 oreo cookies, crushed, and 8 to decorate

- Preheat the oven to 180°C/350°F/Gas Mark 4 and line a cupcake tray with paper cases.
- In a large bowl combine all the dry ingredients except for the chocolate chips. Make a well in the centre of the bowl, break in the 2 eggs and add the butter. Using an electric hand mixer beat all the ingredients together until combined. Add in half the milk/water and beat again until combined. You are looking for the batter to be light and creamy. Add the rest of the liquid in stages as required. Stir through the chocolate chips.
- Divide the batter evenly into the paper cases and place in an oven for 15–20 minutes or until firm and light brown on top.
- Allow to cool on a wire rack before applying the Oreo cream frosting.
- For the Oreo frosting simply beat the cream, vanilla extract and icing sugar until it becomes thick. Gently fold in the Oreo cookie crumbles and spoon the mixture into an icing bag with a large round nozzle. Squeeze the Oreo frosting onto the cupcakes and top with broken cookies.

Baked Pears with Spiced Honey

Baked fruit has to be one of the best ways of enjoying a healthy dessert. These baked pears are no exception, served with a nice dollop of yoghurt – they give the perfect ending to any meal. Try and choose nice big pears with good colour.

Serves 6

6 firm pears, peeled
300ml/10½fl oz apple juice
4 tablespoons of honey
2 teaspoons of cinnamon powder or 1 cinnamon stick
2 star anise
A handful of toasted pecan nuts

- Peel the pears and place upright in a high-sided ovenproof dish.
- Place the apple juice, honey, cinnamon stick and star anise in a small saucepan and bring to the boil over a gentle heat. Simmer the liquid for 2 minutes.
- Pour the golden hot liquid over the pears and bake in the oven at 180°C/350°F/Gas Mark 4 for 25–30 minutes or until soft, basting regularly.
- Serve the pears with some natural yoghurt and sprinkling of toasted pecan nuts.

Pancakes with Caramel Apple Sauce

Makes 12–14 pancakes

Basic Pancake Recipe
110g plain flour
A pinch of salt
2 large eggs
200ml milk
75ml water
2 tablespoons of melted butter

For the sauce:
75g/3oz butter
5 tablespoons of golden syrup
3 golden delicious apples, peeled and cored
1 teaspoon of cinnamon powder
1 tablespoon of caster sugar

- Sieve the flour and salt into a large mixing bowl and with a spoon make a well in the centre. Break the eggs into the well and using a whisk slowly incorporate them with the flour. Don't worry too much about lumps as they should disappear when you add the rest of the liquid.
- Gradually add the milk and water until you have a light batter. Add 2 tablespoons of melted butter to the batter and stir to combine.
- Melt a small knob of butter in a frying pan and add a ladle full of the batter, moving it from side to side until it evenly covers the surface of the pan. Reduce the heat and cook for about a minute each side or until the batter begins to take a nice golden colour.
- **For the sauce:** In a small saucepan bring the butter and golden syrup to the boil. Allow to simmer for approximately 4–5 minutes or until the sauce thickens. Set aside.
- Chop the apples into chunky slices. Melt a knob of butter in a large frying pan over a medium heat and add the apples slices.
- Sprinkle over the cinnamon and caster sugar, toss to combine.
- Fry the apples, tossing every now and then until you get a nice golden colour on all sides and they have become soft (about 3–4 minutes either side).
- When the apples are ready, add them to the butter and golden syrup sauce and stir gently to combine.
- Serve the pancakes with the sauce and some vanilla ice cream.

Kerstin's Bursting Berries with White Chocolate

I picked up this recipe during a stay with the lovely Kerstin from Sweden. You can be guaranteed that if you visit her house for dinner, you will always be fed well. This is one of her classic desserts, which I love – not only is it tasty, it is so easy to make. The tang from the berries combined with the creamy sweetness of the white chocolate makes for a really tasty mouthful!

Serves 4

400g/14oz mixed berries
175g/6oz white chocolate

- Preheat the oven to 200°C/400°F/Gas Mark 6.
- Place the berries in a large baking dish and grate the white chocolate over them evenly.
- Bake in the oven for 5–7 minutes, or until the chocolate has melted with a slight golden tinge to it and the berries are juicy and soft.
- Serve hot and enjoy!

Baked Bananas with Passion Fruit

I don't think I could have written this book without including this recipe. It is my dad's favourite dessert recipe that he always managed to rustle up no matter what we were having for dinner.

Serves 4

4 bananas
4 passion fruit
3 tablespoons of brandy
2 tablespoons of Demerara sugar
A small handful of toasted almond flakes

- Peel the bananas and place in a shallow gratin dish.
- Pour over the brandy and sprinkle with the sugar.
- Cover the dish with tinfoil and bake for 15–20 minutes at 200°C/400°F/ Gas Mark 6.
- While the bananas are baking, slice the passion fruit in half.
- Serve straightaway with a sprinkle of toasted almond flakes and spoon the flesh of the passion fruit halves on top of the bananas.

Wholegrain Apple Granola Crumble

This is a perfect solution for dessert which literally takes a few minutes to prepare. You can knock this together, even if you haven't planned for it. This is my plain apple crumble recipe, but if you have any other fruit hanging around the kitchen feel free to add it. I have regularly made this with mixed berries, bananas, or pears. You can also add some interesting nuts to give an extra crunch to the dessert – try hazelnuts, almonds, or walnuts.

Serves 4

4 cooking apples, peeled and cored
3 tablespoons of soft dark brown sugar
1 teaspoon of cinnamon powder
¼ teaspoon of ground ginger
50g/2oz cold butter
100g/4oz homemade granola (for granola recipe, see page 83)

- Roughly chop the apples and toss them in a large bowl with the brown sugar, cinnamon and ginger.
- Try and make sure each little slice has a nice coating of the mix. Divide the mixture into 4 ramekins or a small baking dish.
- Rub the butter and granola together with your fingers to combine – this can take a little time but just keep on rubbing. Sprinkle the mix over the top of the apple mix.
- Bake in the oven for 15–20 minutes at 180°C/350°F/Gas Mark 4.
- Serve with some vanilla ice cream and devour!

Lemon and Poppy Seed Cake

Poppy seeds give this tangy cake a really interesting texture and colour.

Makes 1 loaf

110g/4oz wholemeal flour
110g/4oz plain flour
100ml/4fl oz natural yoghurt
200g/7oz caster sugar
100ml/4fl oz sunflower oil
2 teaspoons of baking powder
½ teaspoon of salt
1 tablespoon of poppy seeds

3 large eggs
Zest of 2 lemons
½ teaspoon of vanilla extract
Flour to dust the tin

Lemon Icing:
110g/4oz icing sugar
3 tablespoons of lemon juice

- Preheat the oven to 180°C/350°F/Gas Mark 4.
- Grease a 2lb loaf tin (21cm x 11cm x 6cm) with butter, dust with flour or line with baking parchment and set aside.
- Combine the flour, baking powder, salt and poppy seeds in a mixing bowl.
- In another bowl, whisk together the yoghurt, sugar, eggs, lemon zest and vanilla extract. Pour this mixture onto the dry ingredients and whisk well to incorporate.
- With a spatula, fold the sunflower oil into the batter, making sure it is well combined. Pour the batter into the prepared tin and bake for about 50 minutes, or until a skewer inserted in the centre of the loaf comes out clean.
- When the cake is done, remove from the oven and allow to cool in the tin for 5–10 minutes. This gives you time to prepare the tangy lemon icing.
- Combine the sugar and lemon juice until smooth, you may need to add a drop of water or a little more icing sugar to achieve to correct consistency.
- Turn the cake onto a cooling rack and spoon the icing over the top of the cake allowing it to dribble down the sides. Serve in generous slices.

Swedish Cinnamon Buns

Swedish cinnamon buns, or Kanelbulle, were the first thing I learned to bake when I stayed in Sweden. Pearl sugar is sprinkled on top to give it that distinctive finishing touch, but if you can't get your hands on any simply sprinkle a little Demerara sugar to finish.

Makes about 40 Buns

400ml/14fl oz milk
110g/4oz butter
2 x 7g sachets of dried yeast
110g/4oz sugar
750g/1½lbs cream flour
½ teaspoon of salt
4 tablespoons of Pearl sugar

1 egg beaten

For the filling:
110g/4oz butter
90g/3½oz sugar
2 tablespoons of cinnamon

- Melt the butter in a large pot gently on a low heat and then add the milk.
- When the mixture is lukewarm, remove from the heat and add the two sachets of dried yeast, sugar and salt.
- Slowly incorporate the flour one cup at a time; be patient, as the mixture will eventually come together and you won't be left with a sticky mess forever! You may need to add less or more of the flour to get the right consistency.
- When the dough has taken shape and is no longer sticky, turn out onto a floured surface and knead for about 3 minutes.
- Leave the dough to rise in the bowl covered with a damp cloth for 45 minutes. Try and find somewhere warm, as the yeast will do its job a lot quicker.
- While the dough is rising, prepare the filling. Gently melt the butter in a saucepan and add the cinnamon and sugar, making a thick spreadable mixture.
- When the dough has risen, cut it in half and roll it into a rectangle about 5mm thick, and then spread the filling all over.
- Then, from the long side, roll the dough so you get a snail effect and slice into approximately 15–20 pieces. Place the slices in paper wrappers face up and coat with the beaten egg. Repeat the process with the second half of the dough.
- Sprinkle the buns with pearl sugar.
- Bake the rolls in the oven at 220°C/425°F/Gas Mark 7 for about 5–10 minutes or until they turn golden brown. Enjoy!

Blueberry and Apple Nutty Crumble

Berries are ideal for baking, and I love using them in desserts. This nutty topping is so easy to make. The crumble mixture can easily be made ahead of time, just cover it in the bowl and stick in the fridge – ready when you are. I use blueberries, but they can easily be substituted with a pack of frozen mixed berries.

Serves 4–6

50g/2oz rolled oats
560g/1¼lbs cooking apples (about 4–5 large apples)
250g/9oz blueberries
50g/2oz wholemeal flour
50g/2oz butter
6 tablespoons of soft brown sugar
1 teaspoon of cinnamon
A handful of pecan nuts, roughly chopped

- Place the rolled oats, pecans and wholemeal flour in a bowl and using your fingertips combine the dry ingredients with the butter. This takes a few minutes so don't be put off if it doesn't come together immediately. Set aside and prepare the fruit.
- Peel and core the apples, slicing them thinly.
- Toss the sugar and the cinnamon with the apples and blueberries. Be as gentle as possible, as blueberries are quite soft and will easily burst. If they do, it's not the end of the world.
- Spoon the apple and blueberry mix into a small baking dish and top with the nutty crumble mix. If you have a sweet tooth, you can sprinkle an extra bit of sugar on top.
- Bake in the oven for 20–25 minutes at 200°C/400°F/Gas Mark 6.

Peanut Butter Cookies

These are incredibly tasty little cookies which are so easy to make. Perfect for cooking with kids!

Makes approximately 9 cookies

150g/5oz dark brown sugar
60g/2½oz wholemeal flour
150g/5oz crunchy peanut butter (2 heaped tablespoons)
1 large egg

- Place the sugar and flour in a large mixing bowl, and combine. With a wooden spoon create a well in the centre of the bowl and add the egg and peanut butter.
- Beat the egg and peanut butter with the flour and sugar until a thick dough forms. If the dough is too moist simply add a little extra flour.
- Allow the dough to sit in the fridge for about 15 minutes.
- Remove from the fridge and place rounded dessertspoons of the dough onto a greased baking sheet.
- Bake in the oven at 180°C/350°F/Gas Mark 4 for approximately 15 minutes or until the cookies brown slightly.
- Remove from the baking sheet and allow to cool.

Index of recipes

Meat Dishes

Fish Dishes

Rice & Noodle Dishes

Pasta Dishes

Vegetarian Dishes

Desserts

Index of ingredients

Thanks a million to everyone who gave me their thoughts, ideas, criticism and comments. It was amazing to speak to so many people I never thought had an interest in food, who enthusiastically spoke about their favourite recipes and cooking tips.

An absolutely massive thank you to my godmother Erica, who was my sous chef, food stylist, my rent-a-kitchen, proof reader, psychiatrist and so much more. I couldn't have done it without you and sorry for the permanent burn mark this book has left on your brand new kitchen counter. Not to mention the chopping board which now has a lovely smoked look to it!

To the gorgeous Sofie, who gave up so many weekends to help me with the photos. For all the support, love and basically for putting up with every project I come up with and allowing me to follow it through!

A massive thank you to Jocasta for working so hard with me on the photos, for answering all my questions and for teaching me so much!

Huge thanks to Aoife N. for being a great friend and for the amazing action photos in the book. Thanks for spending so much time getting the right shots and for putting up with my posing all these years!

Massive love and thanks to my mom and dad, Liz and Dermot, for supporting me through one wild idea after the next. Thanks for all the opportunities and by the way, thanks to Fresh Cut Foods for that constant supply of fruit and vegetables!

Thanks to James and Michael for giving me the time to write. Hopefully James will learn how to cook at least one recipe from this book! Michael thanks for all the ideas, the harshest criticism and for not killing me.

Thanks to the lady with all the plates, my lovely Auntie Ann, who allowed me to ransack her kitchen for many of the bits and bobs in the photos. Thanks for the constant support and love from both you and Fergus.

To all the bloggers and blog readers who have provided massive support, through both comments and emails.

A huge thank you to my family, grandparents, cousins, aunts, uncles, friends and Angie for all the amazing support, help and for just being there.

A special thanks to Amanda, whose pots and pans got a second life!

Big thanks to all at Mercier Press, especially Eoin, Catherine, Wendy and Patrick who have helped me every step of the way.